Joanna Greaves wanted to write at 18. At 51, it happened. She picked up her pen to write her mum's eulogy and was encouraged by the same English teacher she had at 16, who said, "You have to keep writing!" So indeed she has!

At this turning point of her life, she 'closed the curtain' on a 29-year teaching career to commit herself to achieving her lifetime's ambition. Attending a short 6-hour writing course, then establishing with a friend her own writing group, which she leads weekly in her hometown of Belper, Derbyshire, has allowed her to find her written voice once more.

Her aim is to reach readers who have similar life experiences and wish to read a message of hope and renewal, and also to support the younger versions of herself who may be fighting those same battles and need a glimmer of hope, a sprinkle of joy and a burst of optimism.

This book is dedicated to those who have been in my life journey so far and helped me to arrive at this point. One teacher can shape your future and touch your life more than they will ever realise. That one teacher is why I am writing now. She believed in my writing when I was 16, and when reconnecting with me as a 50-year-old, she simply said, “Keep writing.” I owe it to her to do that, so here we are. This is for you, Edith (Miss Hawley). x

Photographs by John Greaves—my talented dad, who never believed he could…and should have.

Illustrations by Laura England—a former pupil who makes me realise why I taught and is a living example of ‘holding on’ being more than worth it—and Claire Thompson—a winter friend.

Joanna Greaves

Love, Labour and Loss

Austin Macauley Publishers®
London * Cambridge * New York * Sharjah

All of the events in this memoir are true to the best of author's memory. The views expressed in this memoir are solely those of the author.

A CIP catalogue record for this title is available from the British Library.

ISBN 9781037119002 (Paperback)
ISBN 9781037119019 (ePub e-book)

www.austinmacauley.com

First Published 2026
Austin Macauley Publishers Ltd®
1 Canada Square
Canary Wharf
London
E14 5AA

Table of Contents

Be still when you have nothing to say; when genuine passion moves you, say what you've got to say, and say it hot.

DH Lawrence

List of episodes:

Please note that these are not necessarily chronological. Each part has a theme, so if something resonates with you, you may want to only read that part at a particular time.

Prologue

Hope smiles from the threshold of the year to come whispering…it will be happier…

Alfred Tennyson

If I say this book is about **loss,** I fear you won't read it, so as not to be depressed.

If I say this book is about **hope,** I fear you won't read it, so as not to be patronised by the overly optimistic nutter in the corner!

If I say this book is a **memoir,** I fear you won't read it, as you don't know me, and my life is pretty normal, some might say 'boring'.

But this is exactly why you should read it.

I'm not unique; nothing 'stands out' but my experiences (some of which were very dark and traumatic) have always led me to a place of renewal.

How many of us say, 'next year we will be…'? This could be healthier, happier, wealthier. For me… this was always 'to be more content'.

This **can** be the case with an insight into how you work emotionally and an active mindset. There was no magic wand for me, and it wasn't just going to happen.

This started as a book about 'grief' following the heartbreaking death of my dad in 2020, and only 5 years later, my mum was to join him. Both lives were cut short by cancer.

It has become much more than that. Many of us walk around every day, feeling 'lost,' and these losses can look different for all of us.

Mum taught me that there can be no good without evil, no heaven without hell. A photographic image has to have black and white in order for it to be developed, before any colour can appear. Therefore, if we carry these losses, we must also see the potential for renewal.

This book is as much about beginnings as it is endings.

It does tell my story of this thing we call 'life' so far. Yes, it is written by a menopausal woman in the midst of mid-life enlightenment (I will not use the word 'crisis'), who was riddled with ADHD. My voice was stifled for years by a compulsion to strive for the ultimate in everything I do, a workaholic and perfectionist. Allowing me no time to do what I actually wanted to do all along…

So, here I am…

Jeanette Winterson's memoir is entitled *Why Be Happy When You Can Be Normal?*

For me, I offer you a far more fitting title…*Why Be Normal When You Can Be Happy?*

The Make-Up Bag

Mum prepares for what is to be her final 4 weeks of life, relocating from her previous home of 70 years to somewhere new, but safe. In a rational, composed manner, Mum decides what she should pack, in the same way she has approached the majority of her life, in black and white. For me, there would be a cloud of colourful emotions everywhere in glorious technicolour if I were to be in her place. But Mum prioritises just one thing to sort out first: Her make-up case. How can it be that when knowing her time left is short and when ravaged by this awful disease, she would still want to apply her lipstick and mascara?

Is it a mark of optimism Mum has, at times, recently, left hidden? This strong, defiant lady, who is weakening by the day, still cares a lot about looking her best. Maybe also, the daily routine of sitting at her kitchen table after a breakfast of crumpets, applying her make-up, ready for a day where she will certainly not venture out, but hopes for more. Maybe an unexpected visit from an old friend? A surprise knock on the door? This morning routine is one Mum clearly intends to continue in her new home.

Fast forward four weeks, and that beautiful make-up bag remained untouched. Other priorities took over, and the makeup, religiously packed, was never needed. I will never forget how many people commented on Mum's youthful complexion and radiant glow. The makeup was simply not needed. For reasons beyond my understanding, her dying weeks led to a new purpose for mum. The visitors she had once hoped for were now flooding in. Friends from a lifetime, relatives for whom distance had been a separation and more recent soulmates all came to say goodbye. However, laughter, memories and chatter kept her alive, and she simply glowed.

This make-up bag had more symbolism than I could ever have imagined. A physical reminder of what Mum wanted to hold onto. A glamorous 20-year-old, a blooming mum-to-be, a retiree enjoying cruising in her best 'bib and tucker'.

Mum was so much more than what the last days showed. Her frailty was only temporary.

For these reasons and countless more, I intend to honour the woman she was. This is why, for months after losing her, that make-up bag remained untouched. A miniature shrine of what Mum was proud to be.

Mum's Final Journey

Having been a teacher for 29 years and Mum for 21, my priorities and knowledge base have always been how best to start children off on the right track and nurture them at the start of their lives. From September 2024 to March 2025, I was thrown into a journey which taught me more than I could imagine about what can happen at the end of a life, and I learnt as I went along in a haze of confusion, fear and anxiety.

I am sharing my story now as it culminated in the most positive last few weeks of life, but this was more by luck than judgment, and I wish that someone had been able to prepare me for what might be ahead.

Mum had experienced debilitating incontinence for a number of years and put it down to old age. Her symptoms worsened in January 2024, and she kept them hidden, but she was clearly scared in hindsight. Mum was brought up in the war, in a Midlands mining village and her whole life was built on being stoic, not over-talking about any problems and accepting 'your lot'.

Indeed, I remember vividly her saying to me once when I was struggling with my mental health, 'You talk about things too much.' She was right, but that was my way, and this conflict in the way we dealt with life's bumps in the road was something we would need to navigate in the coming months.

In the summer of 2024, she was misdiagnosed with numerous UTIs and given four concurrent courses of antibiotics with no success. I was 'dog-eared' in my determination not to let this go ignored, and in September, I demanded a doctor come and examine Mum at home. Going anywhere with Mum was becoming increasingly like a roll of the roulette wheel, something I daren't risk. She was the first doctor to actually listen, and what she saw alarmed her enough to take action, including hospital checks.

Mum's life savings was under the threshold of £23,000, so I filled out more forms than I have ever done in my life to secure social care funding for her to access care at home. We were blessed with a feisty, brutally honest but hugely compassionate social worker who kept battling for increased funding as mum's condition declined. Money for her living at home was not our main issue or worry, but I can see why it would be for some people.

I was very aware that if I had not been around, Mum would not have been able to action any of this support, and this was (and still is) a real concern for me. Mum, meanwhile, could not get past the fact that she had worked all her life, paying her pension, National Insurance, etc., to watch her accounts dwindle, just to facilitate her living with some dignity and safety at home. Why is it that we plunge all this money into the start of young lives (not that I am saying these crucial early years don't matter), and then just expect that by the age of 80, you have to face the humiliation of admitting you possess less than a certain figure in the bank to even begin to access any funded care?

From that point on, everything moved surreally quickly, but Mum's condition and symptoms worsened sadly at the same rate. We were faced with week after week of scans/tests/appointments at the hospital (each one being a trial and physical effort for Mum, who was by now essentially housebound). Mum was fighting against this and asked me every week where we could go out, but her wonderful determination meant she was reluctant to use a wheelchair or walking frame, and I valued her safety and my sanity too much to risk it. It still makes me sad to know that her last 'outing' was to the local supermarket and not to the countryside, seaside or even Dad's grave in the beautiful surroundings of her much-loved Brinsley, simply yards away.

The levels of anxiety for me (who at this point was still working full-time) and for Mum were incredibly high. Having lost my dad to blood cancer five years ago, we felt overwhelmed by what was to come. Why was it at that time every TV advert I seemed to see was the one focusing on one in two people will succumb to cancer in their lifetime? Of course, these adverts are vital, but not the most sympathetic when I was faced with both parents in this situation. In October, we received the news that we were both expecting but were still devastated.

I am sure most relatives will say that when it is needed, the much-compromised NHS comes into its own. The consultants, nurses, and even porters in the corridors have, in the main, the most astonishing reserve to treat you as if you are the only vulnerable and frightened mum and daughter that they have ever encountered. For that, I will be eternally grateful. When diagnosed, Mum faced with utmost bravery, an operation to remove the bladder tumour (a real ordeal for someone so frail) to not cure her but simply assess the stage of the cancer.

The moment I sat waiting in a room on my own while the team battled to bring her round, sitting beside a Christmas tree was a contradiction I will never forget. But Mum battled on with determination, and this was simply not 'her time'. In many ways, looking back, this point was pivotal and one where I felt I could so easily have lost her. As Gordon (a theatre nurse) came through those double doors to tell me I could meet her downstairs and walk alongside her bed to the ward to recover, she smiled at me, and I don't think I have ever valued and appreciated her more. But it was very much an agonising waiting game then for me, who, as a well-established 'overthinker', went through every possible scenario.

Back home, Mum ploughed on but only due to her Mum's wonderful Personal Assistant (an unknown concept before this but far more preferable to mum's preconceptions of carers) Annie, whose hours had now been increased to a staggering six hours a day. Not only did she care for mum in a way that I never could have, intimately and practically, but she brought mum back to life in many ways. Mum's body was weakening, but her spirit and enjoyment of life within the same four walls were replenished by Annie's spirit, zest for life and wonderful smile. This aspect of social care is one that not many are aware of, a personal assistant that Mum chose, who became a part of our lives very much and enabled myself and Mum to then return to a mother and daughter relationship rather than a mother and reluctant carer.

Had I been Mum's carer (a pressure that many adult children feel), I felt I would have been compromising my own health and family. Amazingly, I now looked forward to my visits with Mum, and we started to bond in a way we hadn't for a long time. As Christmas plans had been put on hold previously, we were now able to buy the Christmas turkey (something I hadn't dared do before), and we were all determined to get mum to our house gently after masses of planning and preparation, to enjoy what we all suspected, but didn't know, would be her last Christmas.

This little bubble of safety and creating memories at home was well and truly 'popped' when Mum was admitted to hospital in January. The original time scale of 1-2 years without treatment soon changed like a lightning bolt from the blue. We were told by a highly skilled consultant (who felt like an angel in human form) and softly spoken palliative care nurse that 'weeks', not years or months, would be all that we had left together. At this point, I knew I couldn't continue to work and process all this, and I wanted to be alongside mum the whole way. It is the only time in my 29-year career when Mum said, "You will be off work, won't you?" and the only time I was willing to do this without question and most importantly, guilt.

We tried to keep Mum at home with her much-loved Annie and district nurse input, but her pain was not being managed effectively enough, and one Tuesday morning, after Mum phoning me in such distress, I decided to look for a nursing home just so I knew she would be **safe.** Being safe is for me the most crucial baseline for both those at the start and end of their lives. Safeguarding is given the highest of priorities in schools, but again, with adults over a certain age, it is as if this just doesn't matter.

Again, no one had fully prepared me for this potential next step. I had a scribbled-down phone number labelled 'Fast track' and rang it in the hope the rest would become clear. I was emailed a list of 100+ homes, and this is where 'luck rather than judgement' played its part once more. I rang the home, which our social worker had encouraged mum to go to on day visits, back in September, for 'social activities and company'. Given that Wren Hall is an award-winning nursing home which predominantly specialises in dementia care, there is only 1 'end-of-life suite'. Heart in mouth, as I rang the number (at this point, completely without Mum's knowledge), Bill answered, and within half an hour, I was about to view the place where Mum would end her life.

I will never forget either Bill's kindness and honesty, as I asked, "Do people actually die in this room?" or the quandary I was in. I had no idea that in the space of a few hours, Mum's plan to die at home would be shaken by me, the one she loved the most, and we would be tearing her from her home of 70 years. No one could help me make this immense decision, as an only child, this was on me alone. The fact that this room was empty seemed to me to be a sign that it was somehow waiting for her.

Being an only child for my 50 years meant that my 'go-tos' in troubled times were my mum and dad. I cannot tell you the number of times they received a phone call or a knock at the door, where they were faced with a crumbling daughter who needed, first and foremost, a hug and secondly, sage advice. This was me, on my own, in a room thinking…what do I do? I did what I had done, the whole way through this…I went with my gut instinct. Had I not done my research, asked the right questions, I know categorically that Mum would have had a very different last few months of life and also know that she would have passed away far sooner. This lottery regarding end-of-life/ palliative care needs to be addressed so that it is less of a game of luck.

I am also fully aware, in this climate of debate regarding assisted dying, that my view has indeed changed. As Mum was at this cusp of moving to Wren Hall, she could (to my knowledge) have made the decision to end her life at that point. She had been told she had only weeks to live; it was terminal cancer, of sound mind, and she was suffering escalating pain and real indignity. Prior to this, I would be the first to fight for our right to end our lives as we wish and be responsible for making our own, informed decisions. But if this had been the case, I, her much-adored granddaughter and countless family and friends would have been denied the priceless chance to be with mum in what was to be her last four weeks.

From day one at Mum's new home, everyone we encountered was incredible. Within a few days, I felt familiar with the home and staff and on every visit, I was greeted with a smile or a wave by all staff. A member of the maintenance team providing me with a kettle, biscuits and milk in the fridge nearly made me cry as these little touches make all the difference when you are on your own. Mum's situation meant that she was quite happy to stay in her room. We spent many happy hours together, watching TV, talking, viewing footage of her favourite holidays, even sharing a takeaway one evening with the rest of the family.

I was committed to visiting every day, and I had scheduled a highly choreographed programme of Mum's nearest and dearest who were to visit over the next few weeks. This was a decision that was to prove crucial in Mum's motivation to keep fighting. She wanted her chance to say goodbye to those she loved, laugh over old times, and look at family photos together. One precious Monday afternoon, I sat on Mum's bed and wrote for a continuous three hours, her eulogy for her funeral and then read it to her. Who could ask for more at the end of her life, to be read what her only daughter felt about her, a six-page memoir of her life well lived?

I had also been blessed by many messages from ex-pupils whose lives Mum had influenced. My primary aim at this point was for her to know exactly how loved she was. Even her much-loved Annie visited in her last week of life after her shift finished at 9:30 pm. Mum, in some ways oblivious to this, but knew deep down she was there. When Mum's minister came on two occasions, staff were particularly respectful and interested in this vital part of the process of Mum 'letting go'.

There were so many moments of magic that happened in this last month. In many ways, in Mum's declining state physically, she came 'alive' in a way we couldn't have believed was possible. Beautiful relationships were formed with a range of staff, from cleaners to the maintenance team, to highly skilled nurses, to the carers. Mum loved lots of the staff and made no bones about telling all her visitors how wonderful they all were. The fact that four of the staff were Mum's former pupils was even more special and seemed very fitting in terms of Mum's life coming full circle. She was not always an easy lady to please, but she also felt valued and able to say when something wasn't to her exacting standards.

I was constantly amazed by the expert knowledge that the nurses showed and how they knew when to escalate medication. I had read about the use of a morphine driver and anticipatory medicines one night in bed when 'death-scrolling', but thank goodness I did, as I was able to ask for this and understand how Mum's condition was worsening. After three full weeks, it came to Mum's last week, and the stream of visitors stopped, as Mum tired. I had started to believe that Mum would carry on this way for many months, so the realisation that Mum was fading brought more anxiety my way.

That said, the continuity of staff whom I trusted completely and again, an honest communication where the office staff relayed my questions or fears, helped the last few days be as special as they could be. Mum was undoubtedly in great pain, and although it was expertly managed, as was her personal care, there was a realisation that death does not always come when you or your loved one thinks it will. We both questioned why, when Mum was ready to pass, she was having to endure so much pain and indignity. In these last precious days, I appreciated Mum and me being left alone, but also knew that someone was only a few steps away if I needed it. Hugs were given when I needed them most.

Mum was still able to laugh, engage with staff and was 'sharp as a button' till the end. When the last day dawned, a call from the home to warn me that Mum was still sleeping and to expect that a turn for the worse was on the cards was appropriately timed and prepared me for the day ahead. I was never left abandoned, although I was on my own, office staff, nurses and carers were there for me at the drop of a hat. I was guided through each hour with such care, and this alleviated any fears for my family or me. Mum's personal care was still undertaken with respect and tenderness.

I will never forget the way that Mum's room was reset with her photos of loved ones on her bed head, her Bible by her side, her beloved cuddly bunny and her holding cross never far from her grasp. The last moments were so incredibly peaceful, and I would not have changed a moment of that passing. After holding her hand and playing her favourite music, I paused it all; the Auden quote, 'stop all the clocks' came immediately to mind.

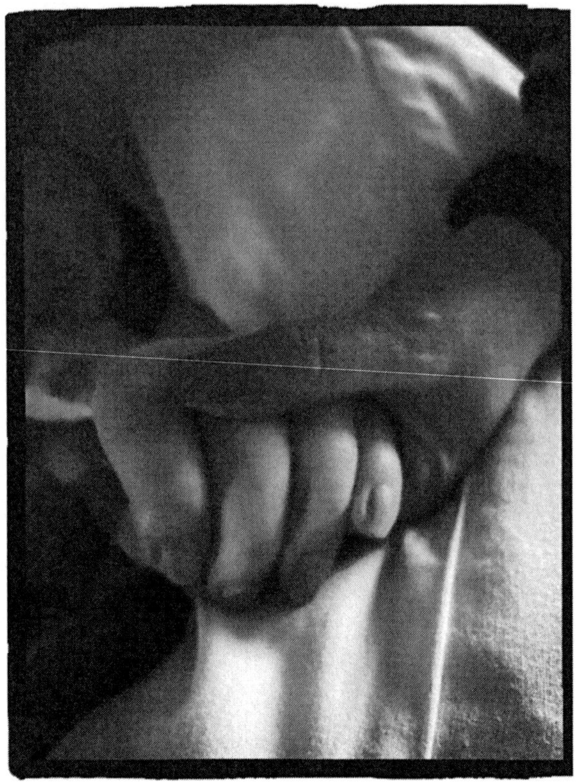

When I looked away, in silence, she took her last breath. I had felt fear at the thought of watching her die, having not been there with Dad in his last moments, but as I thought I knew she had slipped away, I went to hold her cold, swollen hand once more, listened for a breath, watched for some movement and just smiled. Not with joy, of course, or even relief, but a spontaneous smile which radiated from me knowing she was at peace.

The way that the staff attended to me, my daughter and most importantly Mum was with genuine love, tears were shed by us all, which meant such a great deal. The way the nurse in charge spoke to Mum after her passing, in exactly the same way she spoke to her in life, asking Mum's permission to take her pulse, etc, was truly beautiful. The time after Mum had passed was equally precious, and nothing was rushed. This room had become my home for four weeks, and I wasn't ready to leave either. I sat with Mum, her favourite music playing once more, and sobbed, raw, agonising tears.

I could never express fully in words what I experienced in this last season of Mum's life. Some moments will only ever be shared between Mum and me, but will never fade from my psyche, both good and bad, but the way Mum's end-of-life care was managed was instrumental in the way I have managed my grief afterwards. To be able to have fond memories of Mum's last weeks, days, and minutes was something I wasn't expecting. It surpassed all expectations, and I know that she was happy at many points in this last station of life. This has then left me with contentment and peace to be able to move forward without her.

I feel passionately about ensuring that every relative has the opportunity to access what we had the privilege to receive. Having experienced an end-of-life experience that was not like this one, I know this is something that cannot be taken for granted.

I have learnt that death is not always 'pretty' or as we would wish it, and with a particularly aggressive form of cancer, this was not going to be easy. But I know it could not have been managed better.

What more could anyone ask?

Where Do All the Books Go?

Ever since I was small, books have been the one unconditional gift that would be bought for me on a shopping trip, without any notion of being 'spoilt'. This tradition was replicated with my own desire to encourage a love of these 'paperbacks of wonder' in my own daughter. As a teacher, it is almost in our DNA to believe that somehow a full bookshelf equates to good parenting, and if you get that part right, your job to a certain degree is done. I come from a long line of 'readers'.

Mum always had a book on the go; in fact, it was the 'only' hobby her job would allow time for. Dad was known locally as the 'reading bus driver', due to his pausing at bus stops to complete another few pages. My late gran was your typical 'Catherine Cookson gran', but in her later years, failing eyesight led to a newfound craving for audiobooks (in that era, weighty boxes full of cassettes). It is regrettable, that these three figureheads, when coming to the end of their lives, lost their desire to read, as they faded.

It felt as if, at the end of their story, they had filled their minds and lives with as many stories as they could fit in.

Only when the time came to empty my family home did I actually realise just how these thousands of books had almost 'hijacked' the house. There was no place where books were not found: under beds, boxes stacked high in the loft, rammed at the back of wardrobes, the garden shed and perhaps more traditionally, on a grand total of seven 'bursting' bookshelves. It was as if these printed companions had become the fourth silent but dominant member of our family. They had always lived there, but not until it was just me and them did I realise their significance.

A library is centred on the notion of a short-term dalliance, enjoyed but returned for someone else to delight in. This was not what had happened here. If a book had been completed, it would then be hidden away, replaced hastily by a new one. Over time, the new books literally took over and were rarely touched, let alone savoured. This felt like such a waste and almost like I was uncovering evidence of an addiction. A 'binge' of books sourced from a variety of places and over decades of years, which brought instant gratification, but nothing lasting was being gained from it anymore. Now, I love books, and I too would cite a browse round a Waterstones as one of my preferred 'free time' antics.

But to read a book, be educated from it or let it amuse or thrill you and then not pass it on, seemed to be somewhat of a crime. Almost like a child not picked to play on the football team, left on the reserves bench. Equally, if a book which once appealed to me (yes, I have on many occasions 'judged a book by its cover') but was never actually read, then again it was my duty to rehome it with a more suitable family. Whilst books can be beautiful in every way, they can be undervalued and not 'set free' to touch the lives of others.

Learning only recently that some books, donated in good faith to charity shops, are judged instantaneously as if they were on a dating site, and if no one 'fancied' them, then their final destination was to the hell of landfill. Who are we to judge if a book may have reached the end of its life? One person's trash is another person's treasure, and this is what fuels caring villagers to breathe new life into unused telephone boxes with these riches. Donated by passers by to engender a sense of community.

Perhaps I am accrediting too much to these paperback freebies, but I feel certain that when the author, be they Victorian or twenty-first century, slaved away to produce their very own masterpiece, they would not have envisaged such a brutal end to their offspring. The thousands of books I unwittingly inherited from my family home were re-dispersed to future readers, a task that initially felt overwhelming. A small minority had been allocated to certain nearest and dearest in the last few months of Mum's life. Whether they were keen on their new belongings is something I may never know, but boxing up twenty-two Dickens novels to pass to one of Mum's goddaughters, I couldn't help but imagine her response when they were hauled from a car boot to relocate to their new home!

For me, I chose to hold onto a very select few of Mum's 'sacred' texts, and I never dreamt which ones they would be. Not works of fiction, history or romance, plentiful though they were in number. The two texts I kept were dark but true-life stories, which formed a key part of Mum's RE syllabus back in the 80s. *Run Baby Run*: Nicky Cruz and *From Witchcraft to Christ*: Doreen Irvine. Maybe the symbolism of my choosing to retain two accounts of despair to hope, darkness to light, storms to rainbows, is not to be underplayed. All the stories we read (true or not) shape our lives. Some less so, but some will never leave us. Maybe these two books actually chose me...particularly as their appearance was fragile, pages missing from one and the other stuck together with browning Sellotape.

Having had to speed-read a book a day at university, I have always viewed reading a book twice as something I could never justify time for. Perhaps my ADHD, scrambled egg mind, also means I am programmed to finish something, then move on. A task completed, another job ticked. However, with these two books, I have never actually read them. I heard both writers speak at live events as a teenager, but their stories themselves deserve me to pick them up and give them new life, when that charity shop would have certainly cast them aside.

Where do all the stories go that no one picks up, or that someone casts aside, or that never get heard? Everyone's story deserves to be heard. Read on...

First One to See the Sea: Part 1

The feeling of sheer anticipation and excitement when, after a long car journey ('Are we nearly there yet?'), one of our party glimpses the sea. The point where an azure sky meets ocean blue sea, and for a minute, you doubt yourself. Are we actually at the edge of the world? Maybe not the edge of the world, but certainly this water/Earth boundary will forever amaze me.

When 71% of the Earth is water, it makes me wonder why I am so surprised to 'see the sea'. Maybe it is the fact that I originate from the landlocked Midlands, but annual jaunts to the East coast have resulted in a union between seeing the sea and guaranteed happiness. Some childhood holidays were not even booked —the 'hedge your bets' of driving to some seaside town seeking out 'Vacancies' signs, is something I would never have subjected my own child to. I like to plan; I like to look forward to things.

Unplanning for me leads to anxiety.

Unplanning leads to 'What if every sign says No Vacancies?'

Of course, we always found somewhere to lay our heads, but for this burgeoning control freak, we were riding a wave of risk that didn't feel hugely comfortable and was the equivalent of backpacking in my twenties—a thought which never really appealed. Now, I know that comfort zones are relative and mine were narrow compared to families that uproot their lives to tour the world with school-aged children in a bid to educate them beyond the classroom, but for me, this reckless drive away led to an adult compulsion to plan.

When we were safely settled in a guest house reminiscent of something from Fawlty Towers, we were able to relax into our two weeks in the sun. Dad was an artist (with a camera round his neck, rather than a paintbrush), but when it came to sand …well, his talents were unsurpassed! Normally, a speedboat or racing car was meticulously carved out of sand, ready for me to sit in it for the obligatory pose for the snapshot. Another great holiday captured on film! Job done!

Mum and Gran sat in deckchairs reading, aka 'falling asleep'. They didn't quite go as far as a hanky on the head, but very nearly. Gran was one for a bucket hat —long before they became trendy! But these holidays were precious.

For anyone growing up in the 80s, foreign holidays were for celebrities, royalty—on yachts in the south of France. Or on the other end of the spectrum, chips and burgers in Benidorm on a package holiday that would have been as far away from our desires as backpacking! So, when we dared to venture to Malta at the age of 16, I was beyond excited. As an 'artistic, creative' young spirit, my camera now was to capture images that simply took my breath away. A painting or panorama that was so perfect, only God could have painted it himself. Unspoilt by tourism, unspoilt by modern technology, and I was unspoilt by cynicism. This feeling was replicated in my life, only two more times.

Braving the heat of Rome on a bus tour in 40-degree temperatures, the historic icon of the Colosseum greeted us. An image only seen in films or lifted from the text of a page from a book, when seen in reality, spontaneous tears fell from my eyes. Whilst this wasn't strictly by the sea, we were sailing the ocean on a 'spoil yourself once only' holiday on a cruise.

The second time a vista evoked this much emotion was in less exotic Wales, at Portmeirion (the setting used for the iconic *The Prisoner* cult series). This 'Balamory style' (another less cult-like TV show) village with pastel painted houses is the epitome of a 'gated community'. When you enter what could easily feel like a 'theme park', it soon becomes a haven of Italian reminiscence. The bay appears to reach further than the eye can see. To this day, it is quite possibly my favourite place on the planet.

We may no longer be building racing cars out of sand, wearing bucket hats in deckchairs or searching for those 'vacancy' signs, but we are still creating snapshots of memories.

The sea has become much more than somewhere to paddle in; it creates a feeling of freedom, a chance to see something beautiful in glorious technicolour. A vision I will never tire from seeing. Our world is full of beautiful sights, like presents waiting to be unwrapped. But to see these wonders, we need to open our eyes. And how many of us travel through life, without truly opening those eyes of ours.

Snapshots of Time

How can a life change beyond recognition in an instant, but also so slowly, that at times we barely notice it?

Since my mum's cancer prognosis from December to her passing in March, I constantly flipped between feeling shock at how quickly I lost her and then equally, each week of her suffering and us watching felt like interminable months.

Dad was a very talented photographer, who never knew his own worth or aimed high, but his ability to see what others couldn't was replicated in his relationships with those he loved, as much as the images he took. His photos will form a crucial part of this story, him being a narrator of a life well-lived through his images, not words.

Having recently rediscovered thousands of my dad's photographs (like the books, shoved at the back of a loft!), it has led to a flashback of childhood memories which flood back in an overwhelming tsunami. So much has changed. The same Jo, then thirty years later, the same Emma, are still here, but their appearance looks so different, as do the personalities behind them. Images which show complete families are now incomplete. This voyage of rediscovery is bittersweet as I would give anything to be able to jump back into those images, as if I were entering some wardrobe into Narnia.

Photographs have formed such an important part of my childhood into adulthood, a visual record of all that we experienced. But should these images only be of a rosy nature? Photos aren't there to record the times of despair. In a similar way, social media now rarely represents how much we fall short, but focuses on showcasing the 'best' holiday, the 'best' achievements, and the 'best' life. Therefore, the phrase 'the camera never lies' is only partly true. We only reach for our cameras when we see something we want to remember. We are selective in order to preserve our sanity and self-esteem.

I have forced myself to also look at the photos that show times in our pasts that were not our 'best'. For these, too, can shape our futures even more.

Taking a final photo of me holding Mum's dying hand could not have been planned, scheduled, and, in some ways, felt wrong. The agony you might expect to feel at this point when the photo was taken was not there. Only calm, only love, only comfort. The agony comes with looking at it months, years, and decades after. But these images cannot be avoided, even if they cause us pain. If we avoid the photo, we avoid the process of acceptance.

There are other photos that you know were taken, against your better judgment, to mark a 'special occasion' which felt far from special at the time, because what was going on behind the 'smiling face' was mental agony. These photos are a reminder, whenever you take them out of the album, of a time when you were drowning and were 'ticking the boxes' of what you thought you should be doing. Photos were taken to give a fake impression to the outside world. Only a few saw the sadness behind the 'smiling' eyes.

As I have picked up my own camera again, I aim to use it as an opportunity to literally 'frame' my future. For too long have I neglected myself and photos from the past two decades, vary rarely showing a 'me' that was a healthy, motivated and complete version of myself. Then the other years were something indistinct or 'in-between'. The 'indistinct' periods were mediocre, nothing to write home about, but led to a version of myself that I do not want the camera to depict any longer.

At the point of grief, transition and new starts, I was given a unique opportunity to 'reframe' the rest of my life that lies ahead of me. No more putting it off for another time. No more sacrificing myself for others. We are faced with choices all the time. I choose a time when I am no longer ashamed of what the camera snapshot will show.

Every blemish, every imperfection, every bit of the real you is worthy of a snapshot, because it is those flaws and challenges which brought us to this place, and that is surely to be celebrated.

Celebrate the Failures

Please read that again and reflect upon the impact that receiving an identical response from my family, regardless, had on me and my aspirations for the rest of my life.

Probably one of the most influential, powerful things we can do, as parents, but also with other close relationships, is to celebrate 'doing our best'. A failure can be thought of more as a change of plan and a redirection. My parents knew that I had worked relentlessly hard, and for whatever reason, my predicted grades did not quite become a reality, but it was certainly not for the want of trying. This attitude to achievements has shaped me continuously through the years.

Although I didn't know it at the time, being neurodivergent and a perfectionist, I didn't need external pressure. I was more than capable of piling that onto myself. This is a pattern of behaviour that has 'cycled alongside me' in most aspects of my life. As a teacher, I would self-analyse if a lesson hadn't gone as I had planned and use this as a lever to do better the next day. As a parent, I couldn't face the prospect of 'getting it wrong' and tied myself in knots, until being the Mum of an adult, with 22 years practice!

But the ironic thing is, had I achieved those grades on A-level day, my parents would have reacted in the same way, with a celebratory meal. They would not have thought any more of me. Yes, the lower grades may have led to me not studying English and maybe not achieving my dream of being a journalist. But I categorically would not have become a teacher. I had spent much of my first 18 years stating that I would never enter the profession. 'Methinks I doth protest too much!' Without rambling on in a 'sliding doors' fashion, had I not received those A-level results, I would almost certainly not have had the privilege to touch lives and receive many blessings from pupils I now class as friends.

I stepped through the door of a classroom in 1996 and didn't leave that classroom until 2025. Although there were staircases to climb, paving slabs which tripped me up, it was exactly where I needed to be, and I have no regrets.

As a teacher, 'failure' is not a word commonly used in schools and rightly so. It is why pressuring 11-year-olds into sitting a week's worth of tests is universally condemned. But I do believe that part of childhood must involve 'losing' in order to develop resilience and persistence. My mantra with my classes in recent years was that we only learn from making mistakes. Isn't this a mantra that we could all carry with us like a safety blanket through life? We also had a practice of 'fix-its' where the children get personalised support to correct their mistakes. Again, I certainly have needed 'personalised support', be it from friends and family or a trained therapist, to not 'correct' but move on from any mistakes.

That A-level day, there was a greater force in action – I am sure of that. But that was not in our control. What **was** in our control was the way we responded to the change of direction and the motivation we found to move forward. Although my desire to achieve was probably partly in my DNA, I know that my parents' response to celebrate failure was instrumental in why I went on to tick off all the boxes my 29-year career put before me.

We can only learn from the mistakes that we make—let's go with that! If it's good enough for 11-year-olds, it's surely good enough for me!

Sticks and Stones

Something happened to change that wide-eyed, confident, fun-loving girl with pigtails into a self-doubting, anxious teenager whose most dreaded part of the week was Sundays. I couldn't have been alone in having a sinking feeling, particularly on Sunday nights. The fact that I then became a teacher and committed to a lifetime of similar dread is somewhat baffling.

In my teenage years, it robbed me of my whole day. In fact, the only day I remember being happy is Saturdays, when I felt like the real me for a short while.

What was it that happened?

On attending a 'less than reputable' secondary school (which, far from ideally, Mum also taught at), I was somewhat of a jigsaw piece that didn't fit. I started with optimism, having been part of the 'popular' group at primary school. My friend was by my side, and I had no reason to doubt that all would not be well. Sadly, this episode of my life led to a 'loss' of a different kind. A loss of my confidence, self-esteem and ultimately my joy was slowly eroded away.

Twenty per cent of adults state that they were bullied in school, apparently. I'm not here to argue with statistics, but I do know that bullying can vary in severity. No form of bullying, even occasional, is right, of course, but when you are relentlessly subjected to it for years, and it is ignored and brushed under the carpet, its effects are truly life-altering. The attacks to which I was subjected (only ever verbal) took far longer to recover from. Indeed, I would say that, still, to a lesser degree, I can be prone to feeling 'less worthy' than others, a mindset that never existed in me prior to being 11.

Eleven-year-old Joanna wasn't Einstein, but I was bright and incredibly hard-working. Combined with being a teacher's daughter, I guess I was a prime target. That said, I believe (hope) that the same set of factors would not, in today's climate, mark you down as being a potential victim. Other 'reasons' individuals may be bullied have been cited as: being overweight, being underweight, wearing glasses, having freckles—physical judgements made without any other justification. But equally, I have known people to be bullied for being pretty, clever, popular, 'nice'. Whatever the perpetrator's reason, it is never justifiable, and I would argue is almost always down to their insecurities and jealousy.

All this is easy to say as an adult, long removed from the situation, but it was desperately hard to accept when in the midst of it. My 'life glasses' allow me to see it from the perspective of a teacher and a parent, and I know what happened to me was utterly unacceptable and should have been 'stamped out' rather than allowing me to be 'stamped down'.

Daily jibes, whispered taunts and looks of hatred were something I just became used to, only on one occasion, snapping back. How I wished the 51-year-old me could 'do a Dr Who' and teleport back to the classroom where I would confidently and categorically defend myself?

This kind of justice will never be awarded; the only 'comeback' I had was to survive and succeed regardless, even though my inner spirit would always have been diminished to a degree by what happened to me during those three years. I suspect I was not the only one she victimised, but I do wonder how her hatred for those not in her 'inner circle' was allowed to prosper, and with every time it was ignored, her power grew. Yes, there is unresolved anger at how she behaved, but there is more at the system that ignored it.

On reflection, I was reluctant to speak about the true extent of it all. The result of bullying is that it undermines and erodes confidence; therefore, we are even less empowered to use our voices and seek help. One particular lesson is etched in my memory, where a bad situation was made 100 times worse by a teacher who was, at best, ill-considered and at worst, unforgivable. When he uttered, *Why can't everyone be like Joanna?*

In a school culture where it was most definitely **not** cool to be clever, this remark led to increased resentment and further attacks. My parents knew, and I am not here to question their decisions, although moving schools was briefly considered and rejected. Mum's position there as a teacher led to an understandable reluctance to don the 'pushy parent' hat. There was also an element felt by many of 'telling will make it worse'. Having worked in the education system for so long, I do not believe this to be true. Many schools have superb systems in place, such as being a 'telling school', 'circle of friends' and 'restorative justice'. Indeed, I have instigated some of these to great success. Many schools are spot on in admitting that bullying can happen in any school. It is how it is dealt with which matters.

My own experience as a teenager enabled me to work passionately to create a culture where any attacks on others would be dealt with swiftly and with honesty. Sadly, though, the nature of the beast is that these 'predators' know how to stalk silently. They can be clever in disguising their behaviour, and this can be much harder to deal with. The bully I encountered was openly vocal, and it was still ignored.

When I have encountered this as a professional, it has literally broken my heart. I have led assemblies in 'Anti-Bullying Week' where I have laid my story wide open to the pupils sitting before me, sharing my experience in the hope that they will;

- Think twice before treating anyone that way.
- Tell someone if it were happening to them.
- Support someone if they see them suffering.

We must not assume that leaving school ensures the end of our vulnerability. For some, the workplace is also a place where their confidence is eroded, they can feel vulnerable or victimised, and I would argue that this is even harder to address when dealing with adult perpetrators. It is not like you can administer lines or a lunchtime detention! In fact, the same percentage of adults state they have been subjected to workplace bullying as children in school. Karma comes from the success that the victim achieves, whilst the 'bullies' may well continue to repeat their destructive behaviours into adult life. Not that they do not deserve redemption, if they can take into account their own actions and stop the cycle.

I developed a backbone of internal steel, which spurred me onto not being broken by attacks from others. Not that there wouldn't be quiet tears at times, feelings of fear, but I was vehement in not showing it and for every act to undermine, I fought back stronger. What would I advise that teenager or adult who suffered? Just this… If you have ever felt bullied: use your voice and fight back stronger but with actions and deeds, not fists. If you were the bully: just think about how you would feel if someone made a loved one of yours feel that way and turn the mirror back to yourself and how you can make a change. If you were the one watching on: speak up, be brave and be kind. There are countless quotes about how bullying can and must be overcome, but I will close with this thought;

No one can make you feel inferior without your consent

Eleanor Roosevelt

First One to See the Sea: Part 2

The emotions came flooding back as we drove towards North Beach, part of the annual ritual which can never be broken. For years, I have visited this dream of a place, which even in the height of hot summers, feels strangely quiet and still. The large, ivory pebbles fill the sand, a tricky barrier to cross to meet the sea.

Pebbles, which on the most special of visits, I somewhat bossily commanded colleagues and my lovely dad to haul bagfuls of, through the town and back to Derby. These were to form a lasting memento of this day, personally decorated for each one of these 45 (at times unruly) Year 6s, that we had brought to this sea heaven. A place so special to my dad and me, on that one July day, became special in turn to those precious Year 6s and their committed teachers. They devoured fish and chips (or God forbid—sausage!) sat regimentally along the sea wall. Each bite was savoured, accompanied by laughter. The salty, sea air never fails to invigorate but also increase our hunger.

The sight of these bubbly 11-year-olds, 'running lunch off' by embarking on the waves, as if they have been 'set free'. Children, who back home might have been locked on devices, have stressed about SATs results or overconcerned with fallouts with friends, are now running freely, with pure joy and excitement, as if they were toddlers.

This day was simply one of those days, none of us wanted to end and would happily replay it again and again.

To this day, those 11-year-olds, now 27, still recall this school trip above any other and hold those white pebbles close as a reminder of this visit of only freedom and fun, not one of clipboards and knowledge. One such boy chose to take a piece of chalky stone back as a gift to his Mum, which she treasured proudly on the coffee table for years. Much more poignant than a fridge magnet or a stick of unwanted rock.

To this day, those same colleagues are still friends, and one image of North Beach will instantly take them back to a place where they felt privileged to be asked to arrive at school at 6:30 am and return exhausted back to base at 7:30 pm! No quibbles about it being a long day, a wearing journey or stress over unsigned risk assessments. Little did we know that this particular day in 2009 would gain an added poignancy…

A week later, these wonderful images, snapped on that beach, formed an integral part of their leavers' assembly. A slideshow to the tune of Elbow - 'One day like this a year will see me right…for life'. Could there have been a more appropriate choice of anthem for these proverbial 'baby birds'—ready to fledge? As staff and proud parents tried their best to stifle tears, we glanced at our strong, commanding headteacher, sitting humbly on the floor, himself slightly tearful and certainly melancholic. Ask any of us, teachers, parents or pupils if they can remember that day, and everyone will, imprinted on their lives as if it were yesterday. Something that has continued to shape our lives. Because just one week to the day later, we lost that wonderful man who sat on the floor beaming with pride. He was the one to whom we all turned for advice, guidance, inspiration or just a hug.

Receiving a phone call, so unexpected, it rocked us to the core as summer holidays were just beginning. Having been with him just the previous day, where he handed over his keys to his deputy and myself, in what was to become a ceremonial passing on of more than just the keys, for us, there was no preparation for this loss. No warning. Losing a colleague (death in service, it is titled) may not be like losing a family member, but on this occasion, it was no less significant. We were a family, one so strong that none of us wanted anything to change. What a bizarre phrase 'Death in service' is. The vocation of teaching can be all-consuming, and many of us truly give our lives to it, but most don't consider this job to literally take our lives, cut ridiculously short.

To return to the classroom the following September was one of the hardest challenges for us all. Teachers are often described as 'frustrated actors', and on many occasions, I have had to don that mask, hiding my true feelings, pushing them deep inside. That September, planning a fitting memorial service which would truly honour such an inspiring man was a challenge we didn't relish, but were determined to execute to the best of our ability. At that service, grief and loss were not shied away from. There was a raw honesty in that church which was not ashamed about saying how much he was loved.

Two very brave ex-pupils who had recently left the school, had played on that beach, eaten those chips, were stood here now to courageously tell everyone how much they respected, treasured and loved their headteacher. But within this grief, we all knew our lives had been touched by him, and this would never fade, just like those memories made on that beach on that warm summer's day. 'One Day like this…really did see **US** right, for life.'

Those Who Walk by Your Side on the Path...

I have long believed that in life, everything has a season. It has taken me far longer to realise that friendships also have seasons.

Some are an everlasting summer, bringing sunshine into our lives, allowing fruits to blossom and ripen. As with summer, sometimes they can be almost too intense, too much to endure, where all you want to do is escape and seek shade. They can have an effervescent energy, allowing you to get out and explore. However, as the darker evenings come, they can fade, these summer suns are not strong enough to withstand the harshness of winter. Memories of summer do not fade; they still appear bright in our mind's eye and will maybe return for another visit, once in a while. But they are never quite how you remembered them. Like an Indian summer, you try to hold onto them as long as you can, but this is often not meant to be.

Winter friendships have a different beauty, not always visible straight away, but there is an honesty, a fragility to them which strips you, leaving you bare and exposed. These friends are strong and love you in spite of yourself. They are not 'fair-weather' friends. They see you at your most naked and enable you to grow. As a plant is pruned to encourage new growth, so these winter friendships do likewise. That is not to say these relationships don't have fun within them. There is a reason Christmas is in the winter! But like Christmas, these friends are quite literally the gift that keeps on giving…and bring true meaning to each celebration. But more than anything, winter friends are like a warm blanket, enveloping you when you feel a chill. They switch on a light when all you thought you could see was darkness. They will hold your hand when you put that first step onto the ice, when fear makes you feel you will fall crashing down. My winter friends are still here, never leaving me to face a new year alone.

The briefer, fleeting seasons of transition: spring and autumn, come and go.

A brief burst of blossom enters and seems to be a whirlwind thing of beauty, but soon falls to the floor, gently though. No bad feelings or explosive endings, just a natural end.

Autumn leaves change colour, and these friendships can appear to be one thing, but before too long, without you even noticing it, the appearance changes, and it may wither. But there is a beauty there that can be acknowledged and accepted with maturity. These friendships, built as children, can be reassigned to us as adults with a different hue. As fallen leaves on the ground enrich the soil, these reunion friendships can enrich us. They are an unexpected Harvest when we haven't forced the growth; it just happens.

These fleeting friendships need to happen, as they help us move forward to the next season. They shape us, but we can stand alone like an oak tree, proud and independent.

Which friendships would you deem as your spring, summer, autumn and winter friends? Which ones are you happy to welcome back into your calendar? Which friendships will carry you forward?

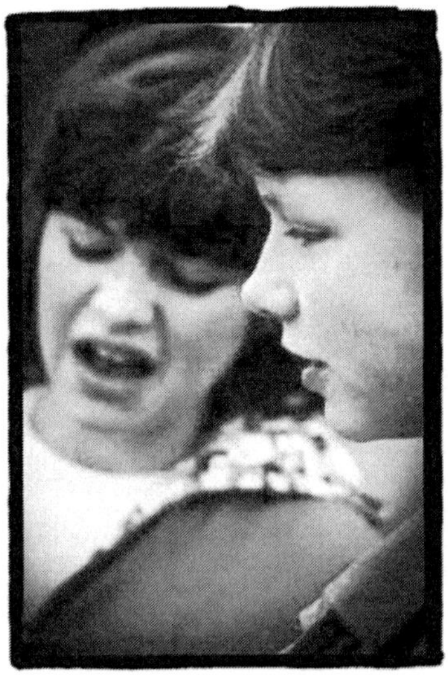

The Angels That Walk Among Us

Angels walk among us; sometimes, the only thing we may not see are the wings upon their backs.

Molly Friederfield

At times of huge trauma, it is fair to say that I have sometimes felt very alone, balancing on the precipice of despair.

But it is also true that I have at times felt protection when I needed it most. In a similar way to how children do not always know what is good for them, when we are floundering in a situation that we cannot escape from, we adults need someone else to step in and decide for us. For me, these are the angels that walk amongst us. Not ones with wings and halos, descending from 'on high' but real people placed into our lives at exactly the right time.

This has been an unexpected gift given to me on a couple of occasions, and the timing could not have been more fortuitous. The first presence of an angel to intervene in my mess proved to be life-changing. The strange chain of coincidences which led to this 'encounter' is almost unbelievable but can only be explained by another force being at work. A positive power which provided this first angel. Whilst recovering at home after my stroke, I had felt immense pressure to return to work, from myself as much as anyone else.

On this particular day, I was due to leave for work to continue with my phased return. The invisible, long-lasting effect which was the most debilitating was chronic exhaustion. On a prior work visit, I had literally rested my head on my office desk and fallen asleep. Sleeping on the job is not something I would make a habit of. I was having to have an 'old-lady nap' every few hours to allow my broken body to get through the day. Exhaustion can often be underplayed in society—how many of us walk around in our daily lives, feeling like our eyes may be open, but every fibre of our body yearns to go to bed?

I was used to feeling tired, but I had only ever experienced the type of exhaustion that makes you feel physically nauseous when having just given birth, now after the stroke and since, in the wonderful period of life that is entitled the menopause!

Seeing exhaustion in someone is not always easy, but my angel was able to have some sixth sense that all was not well beyond my determined exterior. I was about to drive to work, every part of me yearning to just get tucked up on the sofa in front of daytime TV.

My neighbour was literally that, an occasional acquaintance whom we would utter 'good mornings' to, but not someone whom I had spent longer than a few minutes with. I knew she worked full-time time but on this innocuous Tuesday lunchtime, she was off work, quite randomly. This, and the fact that she passed me as I was stumbling to my car, is another bizarre coincidence. She didn't know me—hadn't got any inside knowledge of how my recovery was progressing—or 'not progressing'. But in a split second, she took a cursory glance at me and said, "Should you really be going in to work?"

This short question showed enough concern for me to respond with a spontaneous deluge of sobbing, which lasted near enough an hour. She literally picked me up, held me and took charge. Her actions in 'pausing' my return to work and initiating a longer period of recuperation were much needed, and perhaps it could only have been a 'stranger' who could have done that? I couldn't argue with her, couldn't protest—there was no more strength left in me to fight back. She went into 'crisis management' and contacted the relevant people to ensure I was safe. My primal reaction of constant sobbing had obviously been pushed down into my inner psyche, but one act of kindness from a virtual stranger unscrewed the lid for it all to cascade freely out.

This 'fork in the road' moment could have ended very differently had she not stepped in. I doubt very much I would have reached my destination either literally that day (along the A6!) or metaphorically to the place where I stand before you now.

I can only imagine how wracked with worry my parents would have been at this time, and the gut instinct for a mother to protect her cub never leaves, no matter how old that 'cub' is. Which is perhaps why from this point on, my mum held this friend (yes—she is now an established 'winter friend') in such high regard and called her on more than one occasion—Jo's angel.

Why was she an angel?

*She appeared (mysteriously) at exactly the right time.

* She showed insight and strength of character, which enabled her to make a decision I wasn't well enough to make.

*She showed empathy for the situation I was in and put her own needs/priorities aside to tend to this patient. (Something she has done for me more than once since and has 'dried my tears' on many occasions).

And last but not least…

*She did the best hugs, which provided comfort and demonstrated that this wrecked soul was worthy of care and needed more than a little TLC.

Her presence in my life from that day on was almost certainly guaranteed—no going back to neighbourly nods—a bond never to be broken.

Some angels may be more fleeting and enter a life just momentarily to offer the smallest ounce of comfort, a wise word or a nod in a certain direction. Their purpose is not to be a lasting presence but a 'steer' back onto a path when only an external voice will do.

'Right place, right time' is how some people may think of this. History/news programmes are littered with snippets of heroism, 'moral directors' or 'angels' who were in the 'right place at the right time'. Such as a soldier who was stuck on a ledge in perilous danger, when a climber appeared from nowhere to step in. Such as a driver, tired and struggling to navigate through a snow blizzard, who was blessed with the appearance of a rare car in front of him, so he could follow its lights until the danger had passed. You may have heard of or even experienced these 'angel moments' of your own. Whether you believe these 'messengers', these ‘beacons of hope’ are sent from God is up to you. But for me, if I believe God has a hand on my life, as much in the brokenness as the triumphs—it leads me to know that he must have had a hand in the appearance of these angels too.

Of course, one vital profession is also given the ‘angel’ badge—nurses. For all the right reasons. However, I have encountered the best and worst of these, and the job title alone does not guarantee this blessed title. I will not focus on those who have fallen short. I favour the nurses who have held my hand, radiating warmth and comfort, as I drifted under the power of an anaesthetic, who have reassured me that my future won’t always look like this and have set me on the right path to feel my way through grief.

A whole ‘host’ of angels were present in Mum’s final journey and treated her with tenderness, dignity and respect. These angels are fleeting, but their impact, no less for it.

I believe I have recently encountered another angel, who has quickly become a very treasured friend. Not an angel to ‘save’ me this time—although her appearance was well-timed following a period of healing in grief. I believe this guiding light of a woman has appeared to help me find my voice—to be brave—to take a leap. She ‘radiates’ in a way an angel might with warmth, strength and positivity. Her waters run deep, but this chance meeting, that so nearly didn’t happen, has certainly been instrumental in carving the path you are part of now. The manifestation of this book.

In the absence of the guidance of my parents, I need a champion who will empower and enable me to move forward into another phase of my story. She had an insight into seeing something in this 51-year-old that had been hidden since I was 18. She has helped me to release a ‘gem’ which can shine freely once more, uncovered, and once polished, set free into the world. And I know…another winter friend.

The Voices Inside

In 1890, a wood carver and painter created the first set of Russian nesting dolls. They have since become part of souvenir culture worldwide. I recall my first set adorning my bookshelf, unaware of the symbolism behind these wooden treasures as a young child. Apparently, these are symbols of motherhood, family and descendants. Oh yes—I can see that now! I was fascinated by these 'puzzle' dolls, fitting inside each other, and I would periodically pull them apart and place them side by side, then stack them back inside each other, as if I were tucking them up to sleep. The deeper meaning of these dolls was lost to me at that time.

Fast forward thirty-plus years, and a shop on Steep Hill, Lincoln, sells only these multi-faceted gems. This joy of a shop, rammed with dolls in the guise of Santas, bears, dogs, chickens, and owls! On a return visit to my second home (the uni years!), I couldn't resist purchasing the owl family to proudly place in my office as I embarked on what should have been the pinnacle of my career — headship. Owls chosen by me to signify wisdom—or so I thought. This innocent trinket was put in pride of place in my new office.

From then on, everything 'owl-like' was bought for me from my nearest and dearest as some random sign that I had achieved a place of educational stability. This was not to be, and as darker forces came into play, I left that position and consequently have never wanted to set eyes on another owl again. I have rejected all such trinkets and only now have explored what they could also have signified.

When digging deeper, I discover that there are as many negative connotations with owls as there are positives.

The positive symbolism of owls:

- Wisdom (perhaps owls donning a pair of glasses led to this association).
- Protection (guarding against evil spirits and bringing good luck).

The negative symbolism of owls:

- Predatory (of course, they are programmed to consume their prey).
- Death, misfortune, even witchcraft (the complete antithesis of owls being seen to protect).

Given that I had gifts aplenty bestowed upon me, of owls on cushions, owls on stationery, owls on mugs. etc., I now look back and think, why…? I was innocently thinking my role was to disseminate and promote wisdom, but what if these icons were conjuring up something more sinister? What is it about these trinkets, which are purely innocent decorations for some yet have sinister undertones for others? If we revert to the original meaning of nesting dolls, a mother or teacher producing her 'mini mes', I can see why I was drawn to them, but not when shaped like owls.

Years later having moved onto new educational pastures, I was meandering around the seaside shops when I was bombarded with hundreds of brightly coloured dreamcatchers. I purchased a couple to adorn the willow arch in the eco area of my new friendly village school. These hanging beauties adorned with feathers conjured up thoughts of their heritage from North American culture, and I stared in wonder at their delicacy.

On a deeper level, dreamcatchers are reputed to filter dreams so that the negative is rejected and good dreams will be able to pass through the centre ring and down the feathers to reach the sleeper. If this is true, why the hell did my parents not invest in one for my bedroom as a child?

You see, my dreams have always been colourful! I was once told by a therapist that because I could 'hold it together' so well in the daylight hours (**most** of the time), fears and anxieties would surface at night through my highly imaginative dreams. That could be part of the reason, also the fact that I have always had an excessively vivid imagination, and my job did not always allow for it; therefore, my creative spirit would come out at night.

I'm not about to embark on some in-depth critique of Sigmund Freud's *The Interpretation of Dreams*. The only part of his theory that I relate to on a personal level, is when he states that 'every dream has a connection point to an experience the previous day.' Often, the most minor of mentions of someone or something can be more widely explored in our dreams, undoubtedly. However, with my dreams, there are certain threads/ themes which I have noticed:

- When contemplating decisions about work and my career, I would often dream of my late mentor (whom you met in 'First one to see the sea: Part 2')—as if he were somehow guiding me from beyond the grave. He does not provide answers but positive affirmations of my worth, which will spur me to make a wise decision.
- When working through the loss of a loved one, I would dream of them with reassuring familiarity—playing out every day scenarios. This would leave me to wake, feeling their absence even stronger.
- In times of challenge and adversity, I would experience very dark, sinister dream narratives, which are the polar opposite of my earthly psyche. Nothing I have read, watched or experienced but worthy of a James Bond plotline!

Clearly, when buying that dreamcatcher for the school garden, I should have invested in one for my own bedroom!

The dreamcatcher is also adorned with feathers, another hugely symbolic item. Feathers, in terms of the dreamcatcher, are reputed to encourage positivity. Feathers, in terms of their link to birds and flying, are seen to symbolise freedom. In recent years, feeling a freedom I have not felt since childhood, feathers appearing on my paths have seemed particularly pertinent.

In terms of their spiritual connection, it is widely accepted that white feathers can be seen as a physical manifestation of a spiritual soul no longer with us. What I did not realise is how many grey feathers I had seen after losing my mum, which, unbeknownst to me, symbolised new beginnings, transition and above all…peace.

On this journey from all-seeing owls, to feathers floating from the skies to earth, and my dreams which even the most qualified dream-interpreter or Freud himself would struggle to comprehend—sometimes our 'inner voice' and the symbols placed before us cannot be ignored and indicate that something otherworldly may be accompanying us on this journey which we call…life.

I Shall Not Fear the Evil One

What are your worst fears? From spiders to the dark, or more abstract fears such as fear of loneliness or death, we all have certain buttons which, if pressed, send the heart rate racing and initiate shivers down the spine.

Fear is, according to psychologists, a response to a perceived threat, which protects us and keeps us safe. In that, my fear of heights will ensure that I don't walk a narrow mountain path such as 'striding edge' or 'sharp edge', even though many do. Of course, our capacity for fear and our boundaries differ. So, for some acrophobics (those who fear heights), it might limit them from climbing a ladder, whilst some will manage the ladder but couldn't contemplate a mountain view.

The other facet to fear is that when allowed to grow and multiply, it can take hold of its victim, strangulating them, restricting every decision or option available – to the point where it seriously limits their life. Here, we move into phobia territory, classed as a form of anxiety with excessive 'biochemical reactions'. A phobia is defined as being 'irrational', but our fears to those who feel them, are incredibly rational. In a similar way to how Freud explains the source of our dreams, psychologists would search for either the learned or psychological cause of the phobia.

For me, the sight of an unpredictable slimy frog sitting 'innocently' on my front step will put the fear of God into me, but this is only relatively recent in its existence. If it had not been for a late-night walk home in the rain, up an unlit path, full of the spiteful creatures, I doubt I would have ever considered them as staunch enemies!

Back to that phrase 'put the fear of God into me'. It is a phrase frequently used in a secular society, even though its origins were biblical. When anyone encountered God's power, it often evoked a sense of 'stand still' fear, allowing us mere mortals to feel vulnerable.

This feels somewhat ironic to me, as when facing my worst fears (not frogs or heights now), I sought the presence of God to protect me, not to harm me. In my experience, fear can creep into your previously safe bubble through the introduction of a person who is out to harm you. Not purely a stranger loitering in an alleyway (or other similar scenarios integral to the horror and thriller genre), but an individual whose mindset and outlook are so negative and opposed to your own that they work to block your spirit and erode your will. I am sure we have all had people in our lives whom we have no choice but to 'tolerate', and that is part of the human condition.

Unlike animals, we cannot just devour our predators! However, when these toxic individuals actively work against you to 'bring you down', it can erode the core of even the most positive, confident woman. The unpredictable nature of what they will do next is constantly looming, leaving you with a heightened sense of 'anticipatory anxiety'. This can enter our lives in many different ways. For some, it can be a work colleague. For some, a controlling partner in a relationship turned sour. For some, an obsession held by a stranger who looks in on your life.

I liken this power to that of the school bully who yearns to belittle their voiceless victim. Similarly with adults, their own insecurities or warped desires can allow them to never relinquish their need to 'wipe you out'.

When placed in a situation where you felt fear, that setting can forever 'trigger' those memories for many years later. Just a glance at a building where you were placed in a threatening situation can haunt you—not in the guise of a house on a hill with shattered windows, clothed in darkness, lightning bolts and creaky floorboards—but in a far more mundane form. Fear in everyday life is far more crippling than a Stephen King scenario.

So maybe we need to find an alternative way of approaching fear. Popular culture has developed acronyms to redefine fear. Many are available but I turn to this one: Face Everything And Rise. 52

It would be easy to run away, and at times, this may be what we need to do to protect our physical safety. But with myself, it was important to return to the place I felt the most fear. I felt vulnerable, and it was truly terrifying to 'face everything'. As for 'rising', that may have taken patience and years of recovery to 'truly' rise again. But if we let this entity called fear overcome us, it will keep us from thriving and will still have us in its hold.

History is full of stories, real and created, where a hero overcomes their fears. A skydive to overcome a fear of heights, or a young man with a stammer performing live on TV or celebrities sleeping in a jungle to face those eight-legged creatures which kept them awake at night. All for the sole purpose of entertainment!

On a more serious note, the psychological fields of therapy provide many models of how to 'nail' a fear which is limiting your life. Exposure therapy works on a model of gradually opening yourself up to the fear, repeatedly, until you learn that you ultimately won't die when exposed, and then, in time, will start to face the thing that once terrified you. For me, I don't feel that a weekly date, holding a slimy frog, is essential to my future contentment. However, I did feel that avoiding the classroom, for fear of what it may give me in terms of possible confrontation or anxiety, would have been easy in the short term, but would not have 'served' me or contributed to my recovery.

There was a time when the sound of a phone ringing shook me to my core, taking me back to a time when that sound would signal another problem which I would have to deal with. Now, I can answer an office phone on a daily basis and can deal with whatever it brings, from a place of safety, surrounded by colleagues holding my hand. That particular fear has passed.

For some of us, the most crippling fear we have is that of change. How many of us stick with what we know because it is 'easier' than initiating a change? In the chapter 'Seasons', I explore when we need to judge the right time to draw something to a close. This requires wisdom and discernment. Change is like the antithesis of the comfort blanket we wrap ourselves in. All too easy to stick with what we know. But if we are to face our fears in order to enable us to live, we must welcome change into our lives with open arms. Even if it means we are tentatively wobbly at first, we will, in time, find our feet.

Others fear something far more final and guaranteed…death. This is not to belittle 'thanatophobes', but for me, I have never feared something which I won't be aware of when it happens. Steve Jobs said this about death when dying;

It is life's change agent; it clears out the old to make way for the new.

What a refreshing perspective in some ways! Our world would descend into a mess of overpopulation if we all succeeded in extending our lives through clean living, technological advances and sheer determination to keep going.

However, we sadly don't just die when we are 'old'. My innermost self has never admitted out loud that my fear of losing our only daughter could, at times, have absolutely crippled me. But I had to shelve it, as it felt it was a risk worth taking if I wanted to embrace motherhood.

When fearing death, I have not encountered many children who have openly admitted that they are scared of their own death.

There is a naivety in youth. But between the ages of 4-8, children apparently become more aware of death. As with adults, this fear only needs professional intervention if it starts to limit our life choices. I was fortunate not to have death touch my life until I was an adult, when I lost my wonderful gran. Many have to face the loss of loved ones unnaturally early.

Superb organisations such as Cruse, The Good Grief Trust and Child Bereavement UK shine a guiding light on how we can navigate this with young people, emotionally not yet equipped to process such intense emotions. We may not fear our own deaths on a daily basis, but I doubt there are many of us who don't fear our loved ones leaving us.

In Mum's last weeks, she made peace with everyone she needed to see; she tied up her life with a beautiful ribbon. I coaxed her innermost feelings out of her as she reluctantly and surprisingly admitted she was scared of 'dying'. She knew her Christian faith would settle her into her place, which she believed was heaven, but it was the bit beforehand that she feared. Her last journey ended peacefully, and she had nothing to fear. It turned out that neither did I. The fear of how I thought it would be was far worse than the reality.

Shall we take this belief, to encourage and strengthen us to tackle all our fears head-on? Our minds create a jumbled picture of what might happen to us, but in reality, it may look very different. Just as the 'best' horror films scare you by what is not shown on camera, but what is occurring in the viewer's mind.

We, humans, are stronger than we think, and if we can conquer those who wish to break us, can face death head-on, can change something for the better using our judgement wisely, then I am certain the next time a frog is sat on my step, I can be brave and stand beside it. Who knows, I might even say hello!

Nature's Voice

I have never particularly been at one with nature, but in recent years have started to appreciate how it can speak to us in different ways. Symbolism from living things is centuries, if not millennia old, the Bible being packed with it, from the serpent in Genesis to the dove in Exodus and countless more besides.

In pausing life's treadmill and taking time to look outside the kitchen window, our humble garden has sent me messages when processing loss and accepting new starts. The appearance of a robin is immortalised in modern culture and provides anecdotes following a loss such as; 'When a robin appears, a loved one is near'.

The actual deeper meaning links the robin's appearance in Spring to a message of 'new beginnings, hope and renewal'. Without knowing this, I recall Dad's precious gardening time, accompanied by, in his own words, 'his little mate', who would perch on his spade ready for a chat. So, before even losing Dad, a robin was associated with him. However, now that a robin frequents my garden, he invariably only appears at times when I would have appreciated either Dad's guidance or when I wanted to share something with him. So, that tokenistic phrase, which is emblazoned on candles, grave pots and other items of remembrance, means far more to me than that.

I remain with birds and the collective presence of swallows and their murmuration (what a wonderful word that is!) These are entities with which I have never been too familiar with but again, their symbolism talks of loyalty and homecomings. When losing our beloved headteacher suddenly, as a staff team, we were united in grief, and our bond has lasted for decades since. One of our colleagues used the analogy of us being like a gathering of swallows, where we had lost one of our own but would fly on together to show strength in numbers. Only together would we be able to fly on, and the gap is closed by the remaining swallows filling it. This has always stayed with me, and I will forever be in awe of these murmurations.

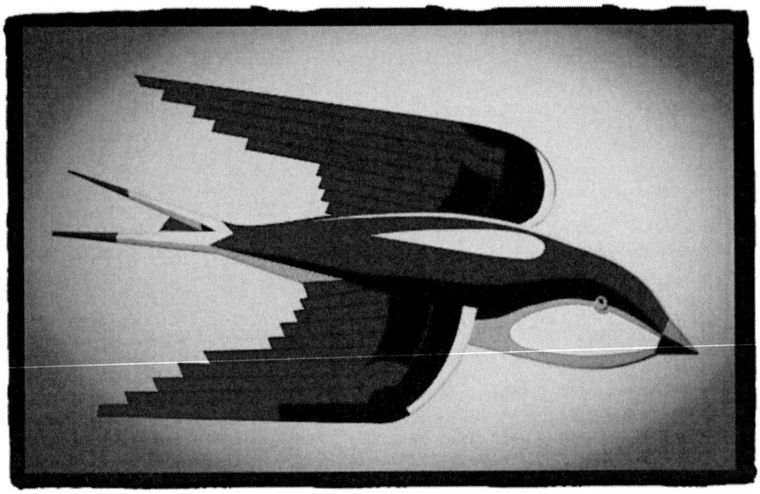

Of course, we could continue to think about other birds and their meanings, but I now move to flowers.

Mum's favourite flower was a red poppy. I have no idea where this originated from, but the fascination ranged from an aged 70s canvas print over the fireplace, to endless kitchen items and trinkets which were emblazoned with these red floral images. Therefore, at her funeral, guests were invited to take a packet of poppy seeds to sow in the hope they would form a constant reminder of her. We have also retained wonderful poppy plants from Dad's garden to transplant like delicate specimens in our own garden, in the hope that they will bloom as strongly as she did and live on. We all know that the poppy is used as a sign of peace and remembrance, particularly of those lost in battle, wars past and present, so I suppose this is fitting for Mum. She was also always at peace, never easily riled and will always be remembered.

Another floral symbol is the forget-me-not which has always been a species, which can pop up anywhere, self-seeding. However, in the spring weeks soon after Mum's death, as we were emptying her house, a flourish of these blue gems appeared in a gravel bed, where they had never grown before. I know this was no accidental coincidence, and from this, I read that both parents were with me, guiding me in how to clear the house, with all its memories, respectfully.

Flowers are hugely symbolic, and we can use them to understand human characteristics and personalities. One of the most interesting interview tasks I have ever been given was to design a question which would encourage a response from its readers on a social media post. I love to be given a creative free rein, and soon my question was set.

'If you were a flower, which would you be and why?'

I encourage you to consider your own responses. For me, I would be a carnation. Slightly jagged around the edges, multi-layered, but when cut, it can bring joy to a room. Make of that what you will! The flowers of human metaphors are endless!

Therefore, we must see the signs nature gives us. Therefore, as a feather tenderly lands in one's path, many of us will see this as a sign of the presence of a lost one, dear to us. A comfort that they remain on a spiritual level. A pragmatic, scientific perspective would rationalise the fallen feather as simply an indicator of a nearby bird getting into a squabble, but this sign provides comfort to many and hope that there is more to life beyond this mortal realm.

What I discovered in the days after Dad's passing, on the same gravel on which the forget-me-nots appeared, would make even the greatest cynic gasp.

I was at my family home, assisting Mum in funeral arrangements, wrapped in a safe Covid bubble. I ventured outside, and my eyes fell on a lump of wood, out of place. What made me pick it up, I do not know, but when I did, there was a gasp of disbelief followed by a smile of wonder and then comfort. This random chunk of wood was shaped as an angel. There was no explanation, but I know it comforted us both, and it sat on Mum's windowsill until she was reunited with him, and now it is safely in my possession. We both firmly believed that random chunk of wood was a message from Dad, even though that cannot be explained.

We don't **need** physical signs (from nature or otherwise) to help us through our grief, but they can help, and it is not for anyone to dismiss something which offers a sense of peace. Who knows if finding a robin sat on your spade, gazing at the swallows above you, forget-me-nots planting themselves, the white feather on your path or a random chunk of wood, is proof of a spiritual guide in our time of need, but until proved otherwise, I for one am happy to be comforted by what nature can gift to us.

A 'Godmother' in Every Sense

A morning which started with monotonous repetition: breakfast in front of the TV, catching the latest news before shooting off to work to beat the rush hour.

Breaking News…no political diatribe, no imminent attack abroad…no celebrity revelations. Just this…

British woman killed in New Zealand car crash.

Instinctively, I knew. This anonymous woman attributed a cursory sentence at the end of a bulletin, was arguably the woman who was one of the most powerful influences on my life.

Val, a little 'pocket rocket' of energy. Somewhat of an eccentric who ignited the room with chatter, positive affirmations and guaranteed laughter. A teacher for a short while, but her identity was far more than that. She was one of those women whose interests, compassionate care for others, and day-to-day life left others exhausted at the very thought.

Mum took Val under her responsible wings, as a young woman, a little 'green round the gills', but needing a little nurture to re-align her. Neither of them is here to recall this, but knowing them both very well, I would surmise that Mum, in her quiet, mature and very responsible manner, took Val into church one day—an event which was to change Val's life forever.

The term 'Godmother' is often flippantly used as a part of a Christening or a baptism, where you may choose an old friend. Traditionally, for a daughter, two women who will 'step in' if ever needed. Life's rich (and not always that rich!) tapestry has taught me that the female role models/sisters I have held on tight to have often come to me later in life. We may all know examples of godparents who never see their godchildren, and it becomes just a name on a dusty certificate hidden somewhere in a drawer. I firmly believe the role of a godmother is one that should be 'earned' and worked on, as with all other relationships. I feel very lucky that both my Godmothers have been steadfast in my life and very worthy of the title.

The term 'Godmother' also assumes some vague link with faith and God. Now, this really is where Val came in…Her faith 'burst' out of her in glorious technicolour, and whatever your beliefs, you could never deny that she was a glowing advert for it! She was renowned for her trademark remark of 'God love ya', and she meant every word!

I owe her a tremendous gratitude for being my 'leave home whilst I sort myself out' person, although it was never actually called upon. I came very close. I have grieved for the fact that since losing her, I have indeed needed that 'go to' person, and they haven't been there.

She knew I loved her; that was simple, but I doubt she ever knew just how much she was a mother to me. It is a heartbreaking irony that she didn't become a Mum herself, but I am sure that I wasn't the only one who viewed her as such, including the impressionable, vulnerable boys she cared for at one period from the Cathedral School. Being a mother to me may not have involved any practicalities, financial obligations or buying me a new winter coat or the like. But she did shower me with numerous affirmations of 'well done', 'proud of you' and 'talk to me, Jo' and the like, wrapped up in her unconditional support.

Some walk into your life when you least expect them. There are those who are only there for a 'season', and there are those who you are lucky enough to be born knowing, who follow you through life. This was Val. Sadly, there are also those who are not destined to grow old, and this, too, was Val. One of Dad's most memorable, well-thumbed books was entitled 'Too Young to Die', featuring the likes of Marilyn, James Dean and many other icons who led a short but hugely dramatic life. Val was no cinema icon, but she did leave quite the impression during her shorter-than-planned time on God's earth.

When someone is taken so suddenly, it is the ones they leave behind who take the weight of the suffering, cloaked in disbelief. I am not sure this ever leaves us and will inevitably cloud our views of believing tomorrow is a certainty. They have no 'preview' of the grief that came as a result of their passing, as my own mum did. Neither do they have a chance to say everything they want to say to those they love, as mum did.

They will never know just how much…

This loss, coming just one month after another influential figure left us, ironically came in a year where I felt at my most secure, self-assured, healthy and confident about my future career path. Perhaps this was why this was the time they both could safely leave me? Time to remove the L-plates and go it alone. A strength within carried me through these two losses, like a steel backbone. What I wasn't to know was that there were times ahead where that steel backbone was not impenetrable, and I would have given anything to have these two 'go to' people back to run to.

Luckily, other 'angels' came into play…

Kintsugi—Celebrating The Cracks: A Pre-Curser

I sit on the cliff edge as tears roll down my face. How could it be that nearly 50 years ago, the man who we have just lost, stood here, contemplating whether to end his life? I was not there, of course, and whilst he was open about the fact that this nearly happened, the details are 'skeleton-like', and I would not assume what thoughts, images, or events led to this. But what I do know is that something stopped him.

Knowing my dad, I have chosen to believe it was God's fatherly hand that led him back from the cliff edge. His time on Earth was certainly not done, and within a few months, a random meeting with my mum at Cliff College during a weekend event sealed a far more healthy, supportive future. His second chance was knocking at the door at Flamborough Head. He just couldn't hear it yet.

Mum and Gran literally took him in their arms and began a slow restoration process that took years. A skeleton of a man came to them broken and damaged. Prepare yourself for a beautiful metaphor I have discovered which can be used to explain trauma being turned into an opportunity for growth. I am in awe of the Japanese art of repairing broken pottery with gold: Kintsugi. This practice creates stunning pieces of art which have had new life breathed into them, to manifest into a piece more beautiful than it was before the cracks appeared. The importance of not hiding the damage or discarding the broken pieces, instead putting them back together, where the cracks are highlighted with the most precious of all metals. This practice is pitched by many as a philosophical way to approach failure or breakages in our own lives.

Dad was split into many parts, and he was grieving the marriage he had lost, feeling shame and guilt at leaving his sons, but knowing, for his own health, a break must be made. But the cracks, his wounds were very raw. He did not feel worthy of love. Hundreds of handwritten letters to Mum conveyed a lack of belief in his own capacity to love again and a self-sabotage not unlike my own at times in my life.

The fact that this was the first and only man my Mum loved was significant beyond measure. She had waited until nearly 30 for this man to enter her world. A single, independent woman, who longed for companionship and hated the thought of 'spinster' being used to describe her, was ready to open her heart to someone who was very flawed.

She had shed tears after friends' weddings; friends becoming mums, and was starting to doubt her deep need to become a mum would ever be a privilege to be granted to her. She was somewhat 'puritanical', it is fair to say: a 'model' daughter and teacher. Dad was prospectively going to be an 'ink blot' on her very pure copybook. Loving him: a divorcee, a smoker, no financial backing or acumen, was never going to be an easy undertaking.

This, too, is kintsugi. Mum took his broken parts, lovingly and gently piecing them back together, and the ensuing 48 years became the gold which she, and then I, painted on. The finished piece was something I was immensely proud of, and even after his death, I could spend all day talking about him and his worth. His light still shines on: through the images he captured, the garden he nurtured and created over decades, and on a good day…hopefully through me.

A Life for a Life

Bleeding and pain, as I entered a class of 7-year-olds one Monday afternoon. Again, the career that had chosen me was dictating my choices in life. I knew something was dreadfully wrong, but had no choice but to hold on—in agony—until 3:20, the end of the school day. I mentally collapsed as I retreated home and hoped and prayed.

You know when life is like pieces of a jigsaw puzzle, and they don't piece together until much further down the line. Well, the first piece of this complex jigsaw puzzle towards motherhood came a few days earlier than this, when my Mum (who was one of the privileged few to know we were expecting our first baby) asked me whilst chatting casually on her sofa, "You do **feel** pregnant, don't you?"

Looking back, this was a bizarre choice of question. How could I know? I've been asked before. "Do you miss having siblings?" Again, how can I miss what I haven't had? So, when Mum asked me if I 'felt pregnant', I didn't know how to respond.

That said, I didn't have any morning sickness, no sore boobs. Ironically, at 19, I had also experienced fear beyond belief at the thought of being pregnant at that age in a relationship which was only 'burgeoning'. That wasn't the case, but it is crazy how our attitudes to becoming a mum can vary so greatly in the space of ten years. This time, it was with my beloved husband—planned, discussed, thought out—not impulsive, reckless or rash. But as we know, it wasn't part of 'the plan'.

When studying for my RE A-level, one particular study had a profound effect on me. I researched at length the moral 'rights and wrongs' of abortion and also the process, from a more black and white scientific perspective. This stayed with me, and my opinions are not relevant; just that this research etched its mark on me. Meaning that I didn't view this pregnancy as cells or even embryos, I viewed it as a baby—our baby. I was not a naïve young woman; I knew 8 weeks was only 8 weeks, but because we had discussed this prospect with such joy, contemplating nurseries, cots, visits to 'Mamas and Papas', this could never be viewed as just a heavy period.

Just as I have learnt in other episodes of my life—knowing is power—but knowing can hurt. If we hadn't known we were pregnant, maybe the loss would not have felt as significant, but it did, and actually, I wouldn't have wanted it any other way. But bear with…

I was low-risk (although 10-20% of first pregnancies end in a loss), in a loving marriage, in our first family home and had a guaranteed support network. But there was a different plan.

This is where we can struggle. How can 'the plan' inflict such raw pain and declare us in some way, 'unfit' to be parents? Were we not ready? Were we not adequate? Was this some punishment for crimes we didn't know we had committed?

No…I don't think so. I am not one for 'hell and damnation'. This episode just wasn't meant to be. We will never know why, but if we can find a reason that feels okay for us and allows us to move on, this is the most we can hope for. One practical theory for me is that my physical body often fails when my spirit won't. We had got married, moved jobs, and I had started suffering from recurrent bouts of tonsillitis, leading to prolonged glandular fever (which, by the way, is one of the most debilitating conditions that is often underplayed).

Ironically, I recall, as if it were yesterday, my dad stepping in as my 'protector' and coming into the doctor's consultation when I was 29, to state, "My daughter is **not** well, and I am not leaving until you give her a blood test!" Nowadays, due to parent confidentiality, I would not be allowed into my daughter's consultations in any capacity, but I am <u>so</u> grateful Dad did. When glandular fever was eventually diagnosed, I crumbled once more and had no choice but to recover. I recovered slowly, but did. However glandular fever attacks the immune system violently and aggressively. Soon after I thought I was fully well, I became pregnant.

It is my belief (my self-constructed truth) that my body was just not ready—not strong enough—not resilient enough to 'hold' a baby. The toll on a woman's body to 'grow' a baby for nine months is insurmountable. I may have thought I was strong, but my body was still physically weak and without any defensive shields. It is no coincidence, but shocking nonetheless, that the same doctor was the one who, in the midst of panic when bleeding months later, provided one of the most irresponsible responses I have ever heard from anyone, let alone a skilled professional. His response when we sought advice, speaking to a pretty vocal, anxious woman, was that the more I 'worked myself up' the more likely it would be that this pregnancy would end badly.

A way with words, he certainly did not possess. I could have taken to my bed for months, and it wouldn't have changed a thing. This pregnancy was not viable. To heap 'blame' on any mum is cruel and completely unfounded, and something that angers me still.

I do not feel that we were the parents of two children, and only one lived. But I did feel grief for what might have been. Grief, and also trauma, for the blood down the toilet, the scan that proved there was no viable baby, the procedure which followed to ironically and brutally 'cleanse' me. How will I ever forget the words that stated an operation to 'remove what was left' would, in fact, increase our chances of conceiving another baby? This felt like a decision that was not really a decision.

A colleague offered words of wisdom when I returned to work less than a week later, stating confidently, "This time next year, you will be parents." She was no clairvoyant but had the courage and faith to say something uplifting at a time when others couldn't face talking about any loss, for their fear of saying the wrong thing restricts them from saying anything. The time she declared this was December, and by the following November, we held our 'bundle of everything' in our arms. Maybe it was unfounded optimism from her, but it gave me hope that this could still be our future.

After a loss, the recommendations were to give my body a rest of three or four clear cycles before trying to conceive again. But my impatience and a healing visit to Paris meant we were not to listen to the medical advice. The pregnancy that followed was anxious at times, but the symptoms missing the first time around were certainly there, throwing up when the toothbrush entered my mouth and yes- the sore boobs! Braxton Hicks became my nemesis with numerous, panicked visits to be checked out, but there was nothing threatening in this pregnancy. The fact that one short pregnancy was 'healed' by the second running its full course meant everything. I had my answer to my prayers.

Once more, she was our kintsugi, and this was the gold over the cracks. But that is not to underplay the loss we felt and the fact that not everyone's loss is healed so easily. We didn't **know** we would be parents, and we didn't **know** we were free of blame. One of the most moving times was when I apologised through floods of tears to my mother-in-law, and I also recall her soothing response, which freed me from any guilt. But it still felt personal that this had happened to us.

As a teacher for six years at that point, who was carving a successful career and nurturing children who needed it most, building wonderful relationships with my pupils, this seemed doubly hard to take. If I couldn't be a parent, then what did that say about me? What was wrong with my body to mean I couldn't keep the baby safe? These questions raced around in my head for many months, but our baby replaced all doubts. This 'wonder' was always meant to be.

All by Myself—Just Wanna be All by Myself

I know the title of the song, epitomised in Bridget Jones' Diary, paints the picture of a lonely woman sitting, drinking herself into oblivion, participating in solo-karaoke. But for me, I long to have my own space, but on my terms.

Having no siblings, I was quite content with adult company and always appeared quite mature as a result of this. I craved time spent with Mum and Dad separately as a young adult. One friend once assumed they were divorced, because I planned outings with one parent at a time. For me, this was because they brought out different sides of me. As a consequence, growing up with adults, I knew I had to work to build strong friendships, and this I certainly did. This resulted in friends over the decades who were arguably closer to me than any sibling could have been, and for that I am grateful, be they spring, summer, autumn or winter friends!

Some of my fondest memories growing up still featured me replicating that solo-karaoke, Bridget Jones style either listening to Spandau Ballet on my treasured record player (as an impressionable 8-year-old, who believed she would marry Martin Kemp!) or devising highly choreographed dances to *Careless Whisper*, which I then forced my family to watch (as an excitable 10-year-old, who also believed she would marry George Michael!).

Equally, as a far older, marginally wiser woman, I sit here now alone, writing. A luxury I have never indulged in since being that young girl. These moments of solitude are viewed as nothing but positive.

This was not always the case. Events that occurred between that joyous girl twirling around at home, to the woman sitting here now, meant that I viewed being alone as a negative, and if I had time to myself, I wasted it, or it failed to live up to expectations. There are times when being alone is 'forced' upon you.

My experience of this for the first time was an unwanted initiation into university life, a small fish in a huge pond, sitting in my even smaller single room, surrounded by strangers. The concept of 'homesickness' is often underestimated and can be massively crippling. It took a good eight months to even vaguely settle, and I can feel the physical pain to this day that I felt after visits home and driving back to return to enforced solitude.

Secondly, after longing for our precious child, having had a 'glowing' pregnancy and a maternity leave filled with emotions I never could have anticipated, I was catapulted into loneliness where I craved the safe company of my husband and parents. Therefore I tried to avoid being alone as much as possible. I dreaded the days when there would be no adult Interactions alongside my wonderful bundle who I just wished could talk. Turns out, once she did start, she never really stopped talking!

Thirdly, within the blink of an eye (the results of an MRI scan), a stroke in my relative youth meant a diary that was crammed with both work commitments and delicately balanced with social engagements, was instantaneously wiped blank. Physical symptoms dictated that I had to stay home, with very little to look forward to and only my own company, whilst the world carried on without me.

And finally, in 2020, some 'little-known' world phenomenon descended upon us, where we were instructed to 'stay home' in some kind of 1984 George Orwell style. For a mother and teenage daughter who were constantly 'on the go' and viewed home simply as a place to sleep, this was hugely traumatic. Whilst we weren't aware at the time that this was due to our shared ADHD; we felt like the rug had been pulled from beneath our increasingly itchy feet, and loneliness enveloped us both once more.

It is in bleak times, such as these, that being alone can result in 'loneliness'. You'll have heard the phrase 'you can feel lonely in a room full of people', and this can indeed be true. I felt it whilst sat in the lecture rooms, the mother and baby groups, the hospital ward and the street full of folks who came out to clap on a Thursday night. Your home, your sanctuary, can end up resembling a prison cell.

I found this massively damaging. Our homes should feel like they represent us, allow us to be the 'real, authentic' versions of ourselves and not somewhere we long to escape from.

Only in this period of my life, abandoned by my parents (through death, not any act of intention, of course), and taking time from a profession which never gave me more than a minute without a thought of a lesson plan, can I now actively 'plan' for time on my own. A friend recently signposted me to a book by Julia Cameron, *The Artist's Way*, where she advocates an artist's date, where we plan time each week to do something that allows us to be creative and 'find our inner youngster'.

If we don't plan some time with ourselves, we don't value our own worth sufficiently. We aren't topping up our tanks and aren't allowing for growth.

When growing older, we can jump from prioritising our parent role, maybe not changing nappies anymore, but ensuring our adult child is nurtured, supported and encouraged in the way we were. Then to those of us who are carers for our ever-fading parents, who became increasingly dependent on us for their every need. Both situations, for which I feel blessed to have had, resulted in a primal need to be alone and properly alone, embracing every moment of grateful solitude.

For it is only when being alone, we can process where we are at, what we need to serve us and where we want to be heading. Being alone now feels like a privilege and one we must treasure, not fear!

Being alone is not one of the losses I am writing about. It has definitely become a gain over the years. In this time of grief and missing those we have 'lost', we must treasure the times we had them with us and what we learnt from them. When friends now talk about times spent with their loved ones, I no longer feel resentment; I feel compelled to tell them to snatch every bit of time they can, as none of us knows when that chance will not be there.

I feel free from the compulsion to be busy all the time. I schedule plenty of time to be on my own and know that this will lead to me feeling ‘complete’—not starved, not wrung out, not compromised—but just me. I have learnt that I am worthy of being alone, just now and then at least.

Right…where’s my diary?

Kintsugi—Celebrating the Cracks: A Lifetime Later

Sat sobbing in the staff toilet at 12:50, thrown into arguably the most challenging Year 6 class I have ever taught, in their last term at primary school. What the hell am I doing? My post-natal hormones have eroded every inch of confidence I previously possessed. A mess of contradictions, I yearned to return to my 'day job', which gave me validation, but guilt at leaving my beautiful daughter at a time when I was drowning. This, combined with a sense of not even feeling as if I was in my own body, was a lethal combination. A few trusted colleagues (soon to become 'winter friends') knew a little of the struggles I was experiencing, but daily life and even breathing felt beyond me.

At times, I dragged myself out of bed, operated throughout the day almost on autopilot, like a robot performing set tasks. At night, I would collapse into bed, not even knowing whether I could wake in the morning and once more repeat this self-destructive routine. In this time of trauma, I sought solace in sleep, but it never delivered what I needed it to. I recall thinking as my head hit the pillow that everything felt so alien—I was lying next to my soulmate, I had a content (most of the time) baby sleeping next door, I had supportive parents who were on hand at a minute's notice, yet…none of this could be enjoyed.

I prayed that one morning I would wake up and feel like other mums…Jesus had healed far more severe casualties than me! But each morning, the same emotions of fear, dread, and despair flooded back with the ring of the alarm, and I put myself through the classroom-based torture once more. I had been told my teaching was good, and others had faith in me, but I had no patience. With the children, yes, I did. With myself, definitely not! Along with 'being in the present', patience was another virtue I was never blessed with. I asked myself the same question every day, "Why can't I just embrace this and enjoy motherhood?"

What I didn't realise at the time was that some things need… just that…time!

If I am faced with a problem, I will strive to fix it before the day is done. Even in recent years, if something stops us from going on holiday, I will make the forceful phone calls summoning the help we need to get us there. If something appeared wrong with my parents' health, I would again make forceful phone calls to demand answers and help. I still swear blind to my daughter that I can fix everything, and if I can't, we know now we can survive the non-fixable.

Hormones, sadly, are a very different ball game—I am no scientist and do not know whether my inability to settle into motherhood was due to:

- Hormones alone
- Hormones plus ADHD traits, where I could not cope with not being in control
- Hormones plus ADHD plus some element of PTSD after losing in my first pregnancy and a traumatic labour with my daughter.

I will never know.

What I did know, though, was that, just as we had covered Dad's broken exterior with gold over many years, a slow process which needed care, acceptance and patience, our wonderful blessing of a daughter would gradually heal my own cracks.

As a teacher, my awareness of how parenting, if you get it wrong, can lead to a sliding scale of mild emotional damage to something far more catastrophic, was something I would internally battle all the time. I constantly questioned if she had eaten enough, was at an appropriate weight, was meeting her developmental goals and ultimately whether she was happy.

My love for her never faltered, ever. My love for myself, constantly.

I was mortified when faced with an NCT class full of breastfeeding mums, and asked how I could warm her milk. Eyes of judgment drilling into my insides and telling me I had already failed.

I was mortified when attending a 'music with mummy' session where photographs were being taken to produce that treasure of a photo we could gift to family, only to literally 'drop' my daughter. Needless to say, the photo was never taken!

I was mortified when changing her nappy on the most designer of changing tables, she rolled and fell to the floor, minutes before I was due to leave for work.

Being told by the hospital, we would have to wait a week to see if there was any permanent damage!

My over-analytical mind, which needed to take back some control, went into overdrive by seeking every opportunity to be a 'worthy' mum.

I bought the monochrome board books for her, which were reputedly going to guarantee your 6-month-old baby would have a high enough IQ to attend Cambridge!

I played 'Mozart for babies' on a constant loop because I had read that it would ensure the mathematical side of her brain developed to its optimum.

I would perform the Sunday ritual of pureeing vitamin-rich vegetables to fill pastel-coloured boxes, because this would ensure she grew to be healthy and athletic (now here, I think I probably got it right!)

I bought every educational toy that would challenge her at each milestone and removed any that would not challenge her, so she was constantly moving forward.

I enrolled on class after class of swimming, gymnastics, cheerleading, trampolining (obviously when she was a little older—she wasn't superhuman!), in the hope that I would be discovering her talents and also socialising her, due to my self-inflicted guilt that she would grow up without siblings.

One particularly dark moment, which Dad carried with him all his life, was when he came to 'rescue' me one night when I couldn't even make sense, couldn't even explain anything, and was emotionally numb. They say, 'you hurt the ones you love the most.' I am not sure I wholly agree with that. I would never have intentionally hurt him, ever. But I did push the ones I loved the most away. He thought he could fix me, and he had to drive back home, in tears, knowing he just couldn't.

Again, his inability to be patient and let time run its course was echoing my frustration, and our antlers clashed. It is why I could look back at photos of him with his beloved granddaughter or him with me, all day, every day, to erase the time when he couldn't fix it.

I recall vividly asking my mum for advice, and although she could be 'critical for my own good' in other areas of my life, her response was simple—'all you need to do is love her'. I didn't believe it was anywhere near as simple as this at the time, but looking at it now as a 51-year-old rather than a 31-year-old, it becomes more believable. At their most vulnerable times, many new mums are bombarded with book after book advising on 'how to mother properly'; therefore, if it were as simple as just providing love, these books would not be bestsellers.

I feel angered that anyone can put this pressure on mums to do better—be it, a nurse at the much dreaded weekly weigh-in at baby clinics, or the doctor who responded with no help or advice when I asked for it, allowing me to suffer on my own or the textbooks that sell in millions with titles such as *The Contented Baby Book* (what about 'the contented' mother book? Where is that one on the shelf?) Or the *What to Expect in the First Year*?' (what you don't bloomin' well expect in the first year is to be hit over the head with a hammer of how you are doing it all 'wrong'!) Or *Calm Parents, Happy Kids* (telling someone who had undiagnosed ADHD and untreated post-natal depression, to be calm is like telling a baby to never cry—simply impossible!). I could go on!

If I could step back into some parenting Tardis, yes, of course, I would have my time again and be more calm, more accepting of the process, less hard on myself and insist on more professional help. Whilst I will hold this period of time for my whole life as something I wouldn't wish on my worst enemy and hope that someone somewhere will identify with these emotions, I actually wouldn't change it.

Why? Because every year she grew older, smiling through it all, she was definitely proving that no damage was being done to her by her hormonally volatile mother. As with my dad, I was slowly appreciating that 'she' was the gold covering my cracks. I had been crippled by depression, which may have 'cracked' me, may have 'cracked' our family at times, but it was never going to 'crack' her. She was growing into a resilient, feisty toddler who would pose for the camera, always have something to say and was one for a social get-together, much like her mum at that age.

Looking back, these are the 'snapshots' I remember now. Every time she smiled, hugged me, laughed, (and very importantly ate all her dinner!) was a gold enhancement on another crack. The kintsugi process went from filling gaping chasms to hairline cracks until the finished article looked like a thing of beauty. The finished piece stood firmer and unbreakable; our relationship was to be tested, of course, through normal toils and tribulations, but we knew we had a bond that would never shatter.

The first 18 months of her life may not have been what the books talked about or what I thought was in 'the plan', but it has been more than outweighed by 20 more years of us learning together and being best friends.

She is, and always will be, my kintsugi, and I hope that I am hers.

He Loves My 'Dark'

One hot summer's evening, an innocuous stroll with someone I had been seeing for a few weeks turned into emotional suicide. I thought that in order to protect myself from future heartbreak, self-sabotage was the only option. I bombarded someone whom I had started to 'get the feels' for (to use a contemporary phrase!) with accusations, assumptions and fears about how it could all end in disaster. I have always been a 'glass half-full' kind of person, but this night, the glass had been drained dry.

I think it is fair to say he was horrified by this emotional barrage, and once I calmed down, he took a fair bit of convincing that I wasn't a complete nutcase and was maybe worth persevering with. This was an incident we both went on to refer to comically throughout our subsequent 27 years, as 'The Cromford Canal Night!' But it was a significant turning point! He had seen my 'dark side' and was still fully strapped in for the ride! And as you have probably gathered by now, it has been a rollercoaster of a ride!

As I have stated before, there is no light without shade. But the times when life has thrown us both a curveball, the dark became, for a while, an overwhelming force.

I wouldn't ever say that I suffered from intrinsic or genetic mental health problems, and I am characteristically an optimist! But life choices that were made in good faith and were eagerly anticipated did result in times of battle where I lost the real me. The root cause may have been hormonal or situational, but both were exacerbated by undiagnosed ADHD, which added another layer of misery. More on this later…

Often, when we are in full-on 'battle to survive mode', we think we are in it alone and push away those who are trying to help us.

As new parents, it was he who crumbled first. He collapsed onto the sofa as we arrived home from the hospital, exhausted after a lengthy and traumatic labour. Yes, my labour, but **he** was the exhausted one! But this is not a criticism; he did bounce back relatively quickly. When we watch those, we love suffer; that love would not be as deep if it didn't take its toll on the observer. During the following challenges of early parenthood, he never left my side emotionally. He held my hand at a Christening celebration where I didn't feel that I was even present. This was a day after a diagnosis of post-natal depression.

On the morning of the Christening, I calmly said to him, "I can't go, you'll have to go on your own." Can you imagine the place I was in to even consider that as an option? This extrovert who loves a party could not bear the thought of being looked at or having to make conversation. Of course, I dug deep, and it happened, but on many occasions, I would have given anything to do it again and treasure how lucky we were and **properly** celebrate.

Daily, he would return home to be passed our daughter, who appeared to loathe 5-7 pm, and although the logical cause was colic, it felt like a judgment and rejection of him. He truly got the rough end of the deal.

Men are allowed to suffer too, and I cannot imagine how he conducted his working day to know he was coming into another metaphorical round with Mike Tyson, when all he wanted to do was relax.

Of course, I know now that post-natal depression was not my fault (although the guilt took many years to diminish), but it certainly was not his either, and he marched on regardless with a stoicism I will forever admire. Men do not always have that safety blanket of friends that they can confide in. The initiative that celebrities like Roman Kemp and Sam Thompson are promoting of the importance of positive mental health for men and sharing their feelings is vital and commendable. We must acknowledge that when you ask, 'Are you ok?'—you need to be more prepared for the real answer you might get.

I do not doubt that my 'rock' of a husband was far from…ok.

I do know that he confided in my mum a few times, in desperation and frail hope that they might know how to 'fix' me. We were not going to give up on our marriage easily and tried to retain ourselves as a couple. I know some people hate the term 'date night', but I believe it saved our marriage. Every two weeks, without fail, we would 'drag' ourselves out as a couple to feel vaguely normal for a couple of hours. Many a night, I declared the same as I did on that Christening morning, but we managed to push through and knew it would 'do us good' even if we weren't in the mood on any level. A bit like 'eating vegetables'.

As with everything else in life, a cliché it may be, but we came out the other side stronger, and it definitely cemented our marriage. Once hormone levels levelled out, combined with a move to our new family's 'forever' home, we were able to move forward to a good place. After a period of calm, we were enjoying our jobs, achieving promotions, forming new neighbourly friendships and more importantly than any of that, raising our funny, ever-smiling, bubbly daughter. As I have said, though undiagnosed, but clearly there, living with two ADHD females cannot have been easy, especially when he is 'so laid back, he is horizontal!'

Be grateful for small mercies, though, as if he wasn't the alpha to my omega, the yin to my yang, we may well have killed each other! I am, of course, joking!

My constant drive for professional excellence led to me securing my first (and thank the Lord) only headship! Again, if he had any doubts, he didn't say, and I felt his pride and that of Mum and Dad and everyone who knew I had worked incredibly hard to get there. The details aren't important, but it is fair to say that the dream soon became a nightmare of catastrophic proportions. Deteriorating health and self–neglect due to overwork led to two medical episodes, the first of which (sepsis) could quite literally have killed me. Appearing from nowhere, but hugely traumatic and resulting in a 'middle of the night' hospital admission, crippling pain, rigors shakes and a massive attack on my immune system.

The second, a few months later, was something that would lead to a complete review of my life and realignment for the sake of my beautiful family. No husband, not yet 40, expects a text message from his wife saying, 'Meet me at the GPs, they want me to be seen by the stroke department.' Strokes I thought were for folks of 83, not 38. In the 'normal' (although we have perhaps established that I am not that!) scheme of things, that's how it should be. Luckily, the lasting physical impact could have been a lot worse, but it was still earth-shaking for those who loved me, as much as it was for me.

A reluctant patient back at home, we reverted to those 'date nights' that had saved us once before. This time, 'date lunches' to bring a modicum of joy to an endless drag of recuperation. You see, in the words of Billy Ocean, 'when the going gets tough, the tough…' Go Out! I have never in 27 years tired of spending time with my 'gentleman'. I yearn for his company and believe I always will. He may not be 'romantic' in a roses kind of way, but small acts of kindness, such as running me a bath on a Friday night after another tough week at school, were far more meaningful and needed.

He is simply my best friend. Alanis Morrisette was our first shared soundtrack, and she is responsible for this chapter's title. She also penned the line 'friends with benefits'. This friend has plenty of 'benefits'. The love he showed to my mum and dad in their last months, weeks and days is worth more than any millionaire could provide. Proof of his unconditional love for me is how he hides his pain when we are in the midst of a storm, but releases it when he knows I am strong enough to handle it. It is then, that I hold him up. There is no greater love than this.

We are a pair of chess pieces. He is the bishop: a wise counsel, moving to protect. I am the knight: known for unconventional thinking, moving in an unexpected pattern. But one is nothing without the other.

I have absolutely no idea how he has managed to embrace my different idiosyncrasies and learned to love my 'dark', but somehow, he has.

I have said to him more than once… "My dad was the best man to walk on this earth…but you come damn close!"

The Life of a Duracell Bunny!

From the minute I open my eyes in the morning…**'On your marks, get set… GO!'**

How much of our 'set up' is genetic or acquired as a result of our environment, both at home and school or work, neurological or self-learnt? In our current society, ADHD (and to a degree, autism) is a term 'banded around' arguably too freely at times. As a teacher, much has changed in 29 years. Even more so since my mum taught those pupils who were in some way 'unteachable'—finding strategies built on trusting relationships that would keep them in the classroom and, on a good day, educate them.

All too often, fidgeting, constant chatter, answering back, and general disengagement were put down to parenting (or lack of it) or worse still, a 'learning disability'— a term I vehemently object to with good reason. In Mum's final weeks, I was privileged to be able to make contact with many of her ex-pupils, some in their seventies themselves. They were keen to send messages about their memories of her and words of thanks to be read by a former colleague at her funeral. What a blessing that she could hear these herself! The influence teachers can have on us is a chapter in itself…but many of these pupils expressing love and thanks to mum were exactly those who were hard to reach, were experiencing problems at home, or those who we would now say had ADHD.

Yet when it came to my own diagnosis at the age of 50, confirming what I had probably known for many years, Mum was somewhat sceptical and took some convincing about how accurate this term was in describing her intelligent, well-behaved daughter. Having always been 'a good girl' who worked hard, was bright (not a genius by any means), but was able to conform to convention, I can see why this was a shock. There was also an element of her feeling 'responsible' in some way and having 'failed'—of course, this was not in any way the case.

It is extensively researched that ADHD in females manifests itself in different ways and can be 'masked' for many years. I am writing not from a stance of extensive research but from personal experience. Since diagnosis, I have been blessed with insight—through new glasses—on how this has shaped me, affected my decisions and been the reason behind much of what has happened in my life.

My journey to this enlightenment started with a mum of an ex-pupil asking me to complete a detailed form about her vivacious, creative 12-year-old, from my perspective as her former teacher. She most certainly did not 'fit' the previous mould of other pupils I had taught with ADHD. However, when completing the form, I was surprised by some of the indicators which were outlined.

- Attachment to adults—seeking praise, affirmations from them rather than peers of their own age.
- High functioning—overly committed to their interests/ passions.

- A tendency to be overly emotional or anxious if plans change or friendships change.

Not just the fidgety, 'ran like a motor' characteristics I had known in boys of this age.

As I filled out the form relating to this beautiful, talented, but yes, spirited girl, I saw my own daughter, but indeed myself. When handing the form over (completed from a place of fondness, not criticism), I knew what I needed to do.

Once you embark on an adult diagnosis, you are potentially opening up mysterious Pandora's Box, disturbing a long-established ants' nest, or poking a very unpredictable bear.

There is no right or wrong about whether a diagnosis **should** be sought, equally whether, if verified, medication **should** be taken. What **is** needed is true honesty from oneself and those who know you best. My mum may have found it hard to accept due to a lack of awareness, which led her to misunderstand what ADHD in females would look like.

My only 'regret' is in not seeking this diagnosis within my dad's lifetime, for I know with true certainty that this was his truth, too. His inability to manage money, need to overspend, hyperemotional, having a daily to-do list, being an early riser and being passionate about his interests to the point of obsession were all traits he and I shared. However, an honest dialogue with Mum about how similar her two most loved ones were, led her to eventually not view this as a negative.

Thankfully, Mum's memory was something that never failed her, so she was able to look back at the pre-teen Joanna, who was a bundle of energy, a natural entertainer, seeking adult company, always 'on the go' and a reluctant sleeper. I recall many a night where an exasperated mum and dad would send me back to bed after my sixth trip down the hall to give them another reason why I couldn't sleep. I also recall (with more sadness) nights in my teenage years, sobbing uncontrollably, Mum adopting the tough love approach, and Dad succumbing with cuddles to try to settle me.

My inability to control these extremes of emotion often led to a pause in breathing (what I now suspect was some form of panic attack), meaning that Mum and Dad would have to deal with me, whether they wanted to or not. I'm not proud to admit that similar behaviour has been present in adult years, with my ever-patient husband taking a similar approach as Mum—wanting to 'leave me be' until morning in the hope that I will have calmed down. The trouble is…my ADHD means I won't settle until whatever the trigger was, had been 'put to bed' or resolved. This can sometimes lead to more self-sabotage, cries for help which won't be left unheard and self-inflicted carnage! I am the first to admit that this version of myself is not pretty!

I found it incredibly hard to look back at childhood behaviours through adult eyes, but it was a revelation to try. I know I was a model pupil; therefore, many of my former teachers would be surprised by this adult diagnosis. However, aside from my extreme emotions, I was also constantly filling my time with numerous interests, with my bedroom reflecting this, but it also reflected a cluttered mind. I had flashbacks to the piles of precariously stacked miscellanea wedged beside my bed or next to my much-loved stereo system. A wardrobe full of clothes randomly 'shoved' in, hidden from view, but lacking any organisation. Every inch of space under the bed, occupied by 'God knows what'.

The feelings of stress this bedroom caused within me, when each weekend I vowed to clear it out, but then, when looking at the task, it was too high a mountain to climb. Therefore, I would not bother. An attitude to hoarding and disorganisation, fed by a denial that both parents clearly shared, if their loft was anything to go by!

Again, this would probably surprise my previous colleagues who have only ever known me to be highly organised, methodical and sure to have ownership of a shipshape classroom with labels on anything that wasn't moving! Those who live with me would say I am still fond of clutter. They may be partially correct. But now, if my mood is affected by the untidiness of my living space, I will tackle it. I will never be a Mrs Hinch figure, and we joke that 'over-cleanliness' makes me come out in hives! However, maturity has taught me that when my traits impact on my mental health, it cannot be ignored.

The most powerful aspect of my diagnosis at 50 was that it gave me reasons why I had acted/reacted as I had to life events. I have accessed professional talking therapies over the years (to varying degrees of success), but none has quite helped me understand myself as much as this diagnosis. With this acceptance came a release from the shackles of guilt. Why? Because I was able to come up with the following equations.

- A predisposition to hormone imbalance + lack of ability to control a situation (ADHD) = post-natal depression.

- A perfectionist streak + a tendency to overwork = a stress-induced stroke.
- A lifetime of racing out the house at 7:20 am, recklessly driving + a passion for teaching, meaning I want every aspect to be fully prepared = 29 years of anxiety-filled mornings.
- A tendency to feel extremes of emotion + a mum and husband who were 'annoyingly' passive and calm = angry Jo!
- An obsessive/addictive nature + a love of food = a cycle of destructive food habits of overeating and extreme dieting.

However, for all of these equations that were not healthy, there were elements of my ADHD that I was able to view as a 'superpower'. Please accept that any tone of self-praise is not arrogance and has taken a lifetime for me to believe.

- A natural ability to teach + a commitment to professional development (completing at least five additional courses) = a successful career of 29 years.
- A tendency to feel extremes of emotion + an emotional awareness/ intelligence = many lasting friendships with friends/ pupils and colleagues.
- An early riser + high levels of motivation = I get things done!
- A perfectionist streak + a creative spirit = when I have a dream, I don't let it go, and this has led to what lies before you on these pages.

Our attitudes to our strengths and weaknesses can only be 'reframed' by ourselves. For every aspect of my ADHD that had the potential to damage, there were as many aspects that have led to success and happiness.

I have reflected on whether an earlier diagnosis would have been preferable, and the only time I think this would have been true is after the birth of my daughter. If I had a label to hang my feelings on, it may have led to greater support from professionals, but I will never know that. The hormonal aspect may still have taken a strong hold, as it did in the menopause, but it maybe would have meant I didn't punish myself as much.

A later-in-life diagnosis was instrumental in my decision to 'draw the curtains' on my teaching career. The early morning hyperactivity is still present (even with medication), but it will not result in me speeding out of the house jam-packed full of anxiety. I can now have a slower sip of my coffee and a 10-minute immersion in cold water—something which has helped me enormously.

For those who have lived and worked with me, primarily, 'I'm sorry'. But only for the times when my internal battery speed has led me to anger or intolerance of others more relaxed behaviours. I will never apologise for my ADHD, as it is starting to be what I like most about myself. But it **does** need managing. My most successful friendships/working relationships have been when paired with someone who is less fast-paced but equally talented and who has never wanted to change me. The yin to the yang and all that! Ironically, post-diagnosis, I have actively sought quiet slots each day and have been the calmest I have ever been. What this can be attributed to is up for debate. Is it…

- Effective medication.
- Opting out of a 9-5 pressured work environment.
- A release from the demands of caring for my parents.
- Or simply…acceptance.

There is still, and always will be, I hope, times where the Duracell bunny is released. I thrive in a busy, social gathering. I often get an extra 'wind' after 12 o'clock at night. I intend to go out 'all guns blazing' at my funeral to the sound of 'Dancing Queen', nothing solemn, still or mundane.

But this bunny is starting to know when she needs to rest. She knows herself and has felt like the light bulb has been turned on after 50 years of blurred confusion.

River Deep, Mountain High

When my rivers run deep, they run really deep. Equally, when I am at the top of the mountain, I am in the clouds!

When self-analysing, words are insufficient. Only this will do:

When analysing my dad…

When analysing my much-loved Mum, husband and daughter…

This is clearly very simplistic, but to a certain degree, hugely accurate.

In days less educated than these, Dad and I's mental 'instability' may have been potentially termed as 'they are very up and down' or 'they are a little unstable' or even worse, bordering on 'bipolar'. I have only learnt since Dad's passing that hoarding is a significant indicator of this condition. But I digress (something we were also very prone to doing!)

I have a pre-disposed tendency to aim for a very high mountain, and this can be followed by a staggeringly deep river. In my 'glass half-full' manner, I now see this as an advantage, a superpower that allows me to achieve my dreams.

Maybe hormones have at times led me up that mountain and plunged me to the depths. However, Dad's DNA was clearly a factor which has also influenced me beyond measure. Those who know/ knew us the best will say we have/had two speeds—80 mph or zero! In the last two weeks of his life, he stopped. Very reluctantly!

A child brought up in the war, he was caned for unacceptable behaviour in school. Despite the fact he was grieving the loss of his father and clearly had ADHD. But only until very recently would any professional have diagnosed either of us. From the moment both of us awoke, we were like bullets from a gun. Much to my mum's dismay, who would happily lie in bed with a cuppa (I was to marry a husband who would do the same!) With Dad, maybe years of shift work led to an 'inbuilt alarm clock', but it was more than this. Not a day would go by without him venturing out to seek constant stimulation: from the camera club, the allotment crew, his 3 'musketeers' with whom he planned train-based escapades, or his committed and amazing choir. He had, like me, a constant 'to-do' list.

There is no hereditary knowledge of Dad's background, due to losing his dad so young and his dad being orphaned. But whether our ADHD traits and behaviour patterns are genetic or learnt is up for debate. What I can vouch for is that I recall our minds being on constant alert.

Dad had the ability to;

- have the mental capacity to read a book at a bus stop for a total of 2 minutes
- toil 'full pelt' in his beloved garden until two weeks before his passing
- feel such extremes of emotions which led him to that cliff edge, and months later to be 'reborn' by meeting Mum at Cliff College

I have the ability to;

- write a 'to-do' list even in my time of healing
- set challenge after challenge so I can 'tick another box'
- feel such extremes of emotions which led me to a layby one dark night, only to feel months later that life was just beginning with the brightest of rainbows

The similarities continue—we were both:

- tidy hoarders—who don't mind chaos in a drawer or a cupboard which we cannot see, but if faced with mess, we will freak
- in an abusive relationship with money, which at best is 'frivolous' and at worst 'reckless'
- erratic and hyperactive, driving those they love to distraction, but can be hugely popular and loved for their passion
- social butterflies, who dominate a room with anecdotes but may be 'flapping' inside, full of self-doubt
- reaching 'burnout' more than once in our lives
- living for the moment

Dad and I may not have looked like carbon copies of each other, but we were made from the same cloth. My physical appearance and choice of career led to relatives at family gatherings utter, "Don't you look like your mum?" But this was a misnomer.

Poetry, romanticism and passion flowed through mine and Dad's bloodstreams. We were both very guilty of using twenty words when five would do. Equally, as much as were had a tendency for impulsive buying, we also impulsively made decisions. Once we had 'set to' on something, there was no veering from that.

Dad was immensely creative, seeing beauty in the most mundane of sights. His ability to capture a view that no one else would have seen was not taught, but was rigorously practised until perfection was achieved. Hours spent in a makeshift but well-equipped darkroom at the back of his garage was where he was committed to his art. I would shadow him, hanging up images to dry, the potent smell of developer liquid almost corroding my lungs! Each image would be manipulated, filtered, re-jigged—the rest of us thinking the job was done. But until (in Dad's eyes), perfection was reached, he would toil away. Like some Yorkshire DH Lawrence, John Betjeman, or LS Lowry, Dad crafted as much as he grafted.

His photos were then meticulously mounted in a simple, signature style and formed numerous exhibitions over the years. Not only do his photos make me gasp with awe and pride, but they are also another example of kintsugi. Why? Because he never picked up a camera until he came to Mum's home, broken. He never owned a camera until he saved money that would previously have been spent on '40 a day's' worth of cigarettes. Clearly, a hobby far more preferable to my god-fearing mum and gran.

But this was not to be his only outlet for his creativity…

I recall Dad showing at best 'a lack of interest' and at worst, 'a revulsion' against the substantial, neglected garden he had inherited. He reluctantly began with an occasional mow and then…the shed appeared. I think we all know what happens to any middle-aged man when a shed appears! What better midlife crisis than this! Not a sports car or a younger model in human form!

Anyhow, gradually Christmas gifts of books by Geoff Hamilton or Alan Titchmarsh started to fuel another channel for his art. This garden became **his** garden, and went from a necessity to a pleasure. Roses were planted, beds were created under his artistic eye, to the point where the grassed lawn became smaller and smaller. He chipped away at it each year to create a larger canvas for the colour schemes he painted.

Memories of hours spent playing in the garden with neighbours and friends, even 'taking occupancy' of a second shed, which became my 'secret' hiding place, are interspersed with solo swings near the magnificent matriarch of an apple tree, where I pondered how simple life seems to be when you are swinging…carefree!

This last bastion of the mark he made when he 'descended' on the bungalow in 1976, would be this spectacular horticultural haven. After losing them both, the house was far easier to say 'thank you and goodbye to' than **his** quintessential English garden, full of rambling plants (much like him!), packed with colour (much like him!) and many areas which grew wild. You know the rest…

So, it is now…when I can reconnect with the 'inherited', 'unrefined' creativity my 'fatherly muse' passed onto me. He always vowed to write his story, but sadly, only late-night conversations or walks in Derbyshire were the only record of this. But his art will live on.

This is **his** story as much as mine…Cheers, Dad!

Halfway Down the Stairs

A poem by AA Milne that I remember vividly from childhood, reread from a brown paperback at my family home. To discover it once more is like a reunion with an old friend. Deep down in my subconscious, I recalled some episode of *The Muppets* where Kermit the Frog sang this. Something so moving and contemplative, sang by a frog! Really…you couldn't write it!

But AA Milne did…and this is what it means to me through adult glasses.

I'm not at the bottom,
I'm not at the top;
So, this is the stair
Where
I always
Stop.

Sitting in the middle, on the fence, not opting for one or the other. How many of us do this? Constantly faced with whether we should go 'all out' and aim high, or whether it is safer to sit in the middle. As I state in 'River Deep, Mountain High', some of us safely drive in the middle lane, whilst others will risk life and limb by speeding above the limit or pressing the brake and stopping completely.

I really identified with a question Heston Blumenthal was asked in his recent, brutally honest and brilliant documentary about his bipolar disorder. He was concerned, as many of us have been, that taking medication to keep him alive would 'dull his creativity'. Something I was definitely concerned about when embarking on ADHD medication. For I would not have been the woman who writes this now if I were not sitting somewhere on a very wide spectrum of unpredictability.

Back to Heston, and his interviewer asked him if he was okay to settle for mediocrity. Before I watched his response, my instinct was for me, 'hell no!'

Mediocrity is my idea of hell. Why this is, I do not know. Part of my chemical setup, my upbringing or events that have spurred me on to prove people wrong? When I viewed his reaction on TV, he knew this was a dreadfully complex decision —I am reading from it that he wanted to live but also had to acknowledge that what led him to success nearly killed him.

So, when we opt for the 'halfway up the stairs', depending on what has happened to us prior to this, maybe it is the safest place to be. But also, maybe we just need to rest there a while until we climb once again to the top.

And all sorts of funny thoughts
Run around my head:
It isn't really anywhere
It's somewhere else instead.

Now, all sorts of funny thoughts are running around my head…here we have another story…

I always had a vivid imagination. I used to think this was because I was an only child, but I know now that this was not the reason. I had definitely grown up drowning in books, stories and dreams, but not in some 'hippy, new-wave way' (sadly!) My dreams were often nightmares. My dad dreamt of pirates, King Arthur's round table, Excalibur and voyages where he risked life and limb, which took him round the world, in his eight hours of sleep. Mum would dream of getting her class register in line and everyday dilemmas. There lies the DNA link, I guess.

If you are not content in your current situation, maybe you would sooner be…

Somewhere else
Instead.

I've known people who live the most mundane of lives working 9-5 (in the words of Dolly Parton!), only to let loose on their two-week holiday each year. This is not for me. If my dreams take me somewhere, it is either to acceptance or to strive to achieve more and make those dreams a reality.

I am…a dreamer! There, I have confessed. But not a dreamer without substance. I know that to achieve my dreams, I must take action. I hope for more, but now accept that what I have and am is enough. To settle in this state of acceptance is not apathy.

Our dreams should always be aspirational. My motto in headship was 'reach for the moon, even if you miss you will land upon the stars'. But if you don't even try to reach high, you are really in trouble! Our imaginations (or motivations) drive us, and this is okay. We need to accept this when our mental health suffers as a result of our 'drive' for the top of those stairs. Equally, if we are sat at the bottom of the stairs, scared to even move, then maybe at some times in our lives…

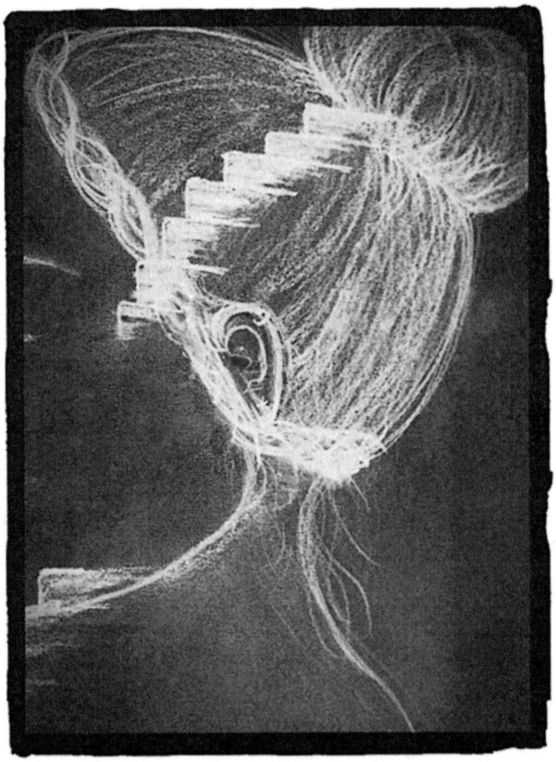

Halfway up the stairs is actually the place we need to be. If not forever, then just for a while.

Wiping the Slate Clean

Any teacher will identify with the first day in a new class and those pristine exercise books where the first page lay pure and inviting, asking to be used: knowledge, freedom of speech or creativity soon to be etched on its pages. I'm still a sucker for a new notebook to write in and have no shame in admitting a secret penchant for stationery. A more philosophical meaning to the first page of an empty book, or in Victorian school life: Wiping the slate clean, is one which has formed the premise of many start-of-year school assemblies.

The official Oxford Dictionary states the meaning of this phrase as 'to forget past disagreements or faults and make a fresh start'. It is also a phrase located in the Bible (Hebrews 10v 17) where it states, 'I'll forever wipe the slate clean of their sins'. Therefore, this reflection will touch on the power of forgiveness, but also the ability we have **every** day to accept the invitation of a fresh start.

As a teacher who has had approximately 700 pupils through her classroom door (although hard to be precise when I've had classes of 40 and classes of 7!), the pupils that I remember the most vividly and who remember me, it appears, are the ones who benefited most from a clean slate that I would give them. We are all flawed—but for children at this crucial age of 9-11, any number of factors can be playing their part. At home, academically or socially, but it can be blooming tough!

Apparently, I was there to hold those pupils' hands when they needed it the most and ensure that in my classroom, they would feel safe to rant and explode one day, but with the knowledge that the next day, I would greet them with a smile and a clean slate. Even when we are 'tortured', surely unintentionally by our pupils (or indeed our own children), if we believe in new starts, this is what we must give them. In my first year of teaching, one such pupil (who I still remember with fondness) slammed the door on my fingers during an episode of extreme anger.

I don't believe this was his fault (upset and hurt though I was), and had I reacted differently, it would have been an abrupt end to a **very** short career. I stepped away, treated my pride and wounded fingers and met him and the rest of the class, with the same 'right then, let's get on with the lesson'. He had multiple complex needs, was not suited to a mainstream setting and for me it was a baptism of fire, but I wouldn't have changed it. He only had me as a safe space at that point in time, and I couldn't opt out of that.

As a parent, I knew I never wanted to resort to slapping or smacking someone I loved. They wouldn't learn, if that was my way of teaching. I acknowledge there are other schools of thought, but it is not my way. As a parent and a teacher, it is my duty to rise above and to continue to forgive and move forward, in hope of a day when that new exercise book is written in and not thrown across a room.

As an adult, you will know by now that I have needed many clean slates myself. Had my life been written over the earlier scribbles, nothing would be legible, a blurry mess of guilt, mistakes or anger. But we are **all** still learning, and if our 'scribbled behaviour' is not intentionally hurting anyone, we have no choice but to wipe the slate clean. If we do not, most of us mere mortals will be condemned to a life of regret, guilt and repeated behaviour. This is not to say I am naïve about human nature and the fact that some souls cannot be saved because they are not seeking a clean slate and therefore do not deserve one. But this is not for me to make that judgment call.

I was exposed by my religious but also highly knowledgeable RE teacher mother to the story of Nicky Cruz. On reflection, I was maybe a little young to hear about knife crime on New York streets, devil worship and a life where he was reputably 'destined for prison, the electric chair or hell' according to a psychiatrist. However, his natural ability to captivate an audience with his public speaking and power to overcome a horrendous upbringing, with the sole aim of allowing others to hear his message of forgiveness was something that has stayed with me for a lifetime.

Why? I do not know. I was no gangster, had no such upbringing, but to know that even the 'worst choices' could lead to a clean slate was something I clearly knew I would need in my emotional toolbox.

Nicky Cruz met one man who was willing to show relentless love. What a phrase that is, and what love it holds within it. In his own words, he states, *It's a love that chases us down, even when we are lost and broken.* This lesson is one for us all, not just those with a religious faith.

For some of us, it may not be God that saves us, but that magic person steps in at the right time to teach us that 'good' can be our saviour. For Nicky Cruz, it was Dave Wilkerson, a street preacher. For more mundane scenarios, it may be that one teacher, Godparent, boxing coach, trusted friend or similar who appears just at the right time. I have been blessed with many of these, and they reminded me (unknowingly) of Nicky Cruz's message.

At times where I have felt at my most vulnerable, in need of guidance, I have turned to my 'elders', either previous teachers or figures in my life who are pillars of faith: My warm and kind second godmother, my very wise and gentle previous English teacher, a dear friend who radiates faith and who came to pray with Mum in her last weeks, two of Mum's closest friends who offered me sage advice and support, showing insight and love. We all have people like this in our lives and need to know that they are there when we need them, and sometimes, reaching out and seeking them in our lives is required in order to get us back on track.

I have been blessed with numerous pupils in my life whom I would now call friends. I know this is not expected when those 10-year-olds are in your classroom, but some souls are worth holding onto. There may be more than 20 years difference in age between us, but similarities such as our ADHD, our fragility and strength in terms of mental wellness and grief, have all drawn me back to these special pupils. Indeed, some former pupils have just 'appeared' numerous times when I needed that hug or words of affirmation, when leaving my much-loved career.

Other pupils have reached out, laying their souls bare at times of crisis—a privilege to be let back into their world, at a vulnerable time. One pupil shadowed me in the classroom for a year to enable her to pursue her childhood dream of becoming a teacher. This was enormously rewarding to feel I was playing a small part in her future, even at the age of 23. In doing this, it regenerated our friendship as we got to know each other as adults.

If a special relationship is built in our formative stages of life, it will always be remembered, and it can provide a haven we can return to in times of challenge.

I know that I could not 'fix' every pupil that passed through my classroom doors, even if I passed them that 'clean slate'. Other factors, as they moved through life, meant that their story may not have ended happily. But I know that I wouldn't have changed the teacher I was, and building positive relationships was behind it all.

If we are willing to give others a clean slate, we must also be willing to give ourselves one at times in our lives when we need to 'go easy'. Each day given to us is a chance to right any wrongs, change our mindset, and decide what we want written on that blank page.

Jeremiah 29 v 11

As I lay alone in my hospital room, a mobile phone which had previously been a bringer of anxiety—the bearer of bad news, a seed of doubt or worry planted by a text, holding within it, a packed diary…lit up with a different message. It was to be instrumental in what was to follow next. It came from an ex-colleague and friend.

For I know the plans I have for you…plans to prosper you and not to harm you, plans to give you a hope and a future.

Words that brought immediate comfort but may have been hard to fully accept at the time. Hours later, another ex-colleague and friend sent exactly the same lines of scripture. These are the times when you know that there is something more powerful at work in the universe than our humble selves. One text could be acknowledged but easily forgotten. But this second knock at my door could not be ignored. I had to listen. From that point on, when faced with such uncertainty about my own future, these words were to accompany me along life's path, in the same way as my winter friends have.

As I have recounted before, good is counterposed with evil, hope is counterposed with despair and words of love (such as these) are counterposed with words of hatred. I had been the subject of emotional attacks on my integrity, and this had injured me physically. These words from a prophet, written in the sixth/seventh century BC, were still to have relevance to a very real context in the twenty-first century.

For those who did not have an RE teacher as a mother, a prophet foretells the future and acts as an intermediary for God, through visions and dreams, which are then shared with others. These two friends, sending the same words, in their own way, were acting as prophets. They were passing on something they believed to be true.

At a time when fear was rife and could have crippled me, anger could have taken hold, or retaliation could have been sought, I was remarkably able to rest in these words. No harm would now come to me. It already had, but I was still standing—just. I may have been slightly broken, but not beyond repair. We are back to our kintsugi bowl! I could now choose how I reacted to this. But I most definitely was not the one in control! The one in the driving seat had 'steered' me here, to this hospital bed, to give me a hope and a future. During my stay in the hospital, I felt protected, wrapped up in a cocoon of prayer and hope.

Whilst I believe that there are 'plans' for us, I also believe that we have to be active in this.

If it is in 'the plan' for you to win the lottery, you have to buy a ticket.

If it is in 'the plan' for you to run a marathon, you have to buy the trainers.

If it was in 'the plan' for me not to be harmed—I needed to take heed of these words and rest, recover and then be led to a better future filled with hope.

Apathy is my least favourite characteristic. If you are apathetic, you may respond with 'What will be, will be' or worse still, 'Whatever!'

I know there is 'a plan' for me, but that would fuel my fire to take this broken bowl and, with help, mend it.

Plans to prosper you—'prosperity' has two dictionary definitions. The first is thought of in terms of money and financial stability. In this sense, I feel compelled to come clean and own up to the fact that I and money can be a lethal combination. I passionately believe that you shouldn't expect money and have been raised to work hard for every penny. However, **keeping** money is not as easy for me as **earning** it. Being in a job at the time, where I was financially comfortable, but where I was too exhausted, too drained to even notice the number on the bank balance, let alone enjoy it. So, in this first sense of 'prosperity', this was definitely not what I was experiencing.

The alternative meaning is to 'make successful', and the Oxford English Dictionary actually cites as its example for this meaning: 'God has wonderfully prospered his nation.' Surely then, this is what Jeremiah meant for me.

But I was successful in my career, constantly driven to achieve more. Qualifications gained, courses completed and reaching the top of a ladder I had never wanted to climb in the first place. Maybe I needed to seek success in other areas of my life.

I may hold the record for the shortest course of CBT (Cognitive Behavioural Therapy) ever completed. It took two sessions for me to realise that, in terms of what I valued (I seem to remember drawing concentric rings and placing work, friends, interests, family, fitness, etc, in different rings according to their worth), work was not my driving force after all. I was enlightened by this paper exercise to the point where I was to walk away from any more stress, but far less monetary prosperity.

I was determined to find 'success' and 'prosperity' in terms of my role as a wife, daughter and mother. I needed to be more 'successful' in being the healthiest version of myself, having been given a warning that I should not ignore. I was to become 'successful' in my career again, but it would take a very different form from how it appeared before, and it would take time.

If I were to 'prosper' …

I would have to listen to the words on my mobile phone.

I had to trust 'the plan'.

I had to wait for the future to reveal its hope.

And indeed, it did…

Women of a Certain Age

A feeling of another overwhelming presence taking over your body, which you desperately try to fight against with every power within you, you grip hold of an edge which may, if your hands let go, send you spinning into insanity.

Age as a number has never bothered me; instead of dreading turning 40, passing 50 and crawling towards 60, I have taken these milestones as opportunities to celebrate. Any excuse for a party! I have never used age as a marker for things. Maybe this is why this key episode of every woman's life came upon me relatively unnoticed at first. I am normally very aware of my emotional fluctuations, which have led to me being somewhat volatile at some points in my life. This beast came stealth-like, its appearance changing from pure despair to sheer exhaustion, but predominantly an emotion far less familiar to me—anger! This sounds like a cliché, but it is one many women will understand. I had a **very** short fuse.

For a teacher who is surrounded by a day full of noise, not necessarily disruptive noise but chatter, questioning, laughter and occasional sobbing (not me, I hasten to add!)—the noise intolerance I had acquired was far from ideal. Even from the safety of my domestic walls, if my two lovelies were speaking at the same time as the radio hummed in the background or birds were chirping outside, I could reach a pinnacle of fury unbounded. It was as if my eardrums, which had served me well for 49 years, were now enormous loudhailers creating a sound comparable to a vuvuzela!

I may sound somewhat arrogant here, but I will risk it. I have been known as a calm presence in the classroom, 'full-on' but not loud, and I like a place of learning to be ordered, organised and therefore content for all those within it. I really knew I was in trouble on two occasions in the workplace. Once, when I looked down at my desk, in front of 10 ready and waiting children, I saw a muddle of Maths sheets, which would normally be meticulously organised. I simply thought, *What on earth am I doing*?

That Maths lesson would never have happened had it not been for my insightful student teacher, who stepped in when she saw the sheer look of panic on my face. Secondly, I could not cope with any aspect of the school day being changed. Now, in a small village school, this is a common occurrence, but it would throw me into the closest I have ever come to a panic attack. I was not a novice, I had been that teacher who took 45 Y6 children to Bridlington in May when they had, quite frankly, had enough.

But here I was in a place where I couldn't function. Yes…I was in trouble! Maybe we don't know what has come upon us until it attacks the best of us. For me, the dealbreaker was when I couldn't teach.

Previous symptoms were probably passed off as something else, namely grief at losing my beloved dad, anxiety about the Mum left behind, post-Covid numbness and a 'return' to normal life. I am eternally grateful that my family 'tolerated' this change in me, having witnessed far worse in the past—but this meant that with hindsight, I was probably only diagnosed with being menopausal about five years later. No perimenopause for me! I was well and truly 'up to my neck' in the menopause, according to the blood test which proved it.

Maybe it was the fact that Mum was of a generation where hormones were a slightly 'dirty' word. I have to take her word as gospel that this 'phenomenon' did not hit her in any way, shape or form. As with post-natal depression, I was starting to lean into, 'this is only happening to me'.

Thankfully (not that I would wish this 'takeover of body and mind' on my worst enemy), my close friends were not far behind me. It is hard when you are suffering not to take it out on the ones you love the most. I knew my two at home could not possibly empathise. My closest circle of 'sisters' may have reached this point at slightly different points in their lives than I, but their suffering was very real. I am quite literally an 'open book', and I remember going out one night with these friends. I sat there feeling completely out of sorts, desperately whinging, easily irritated (if only by the uncomfortable wooden chair I was sitting on) and desperate to retreat to my bed. Again, this was not Jo. It was this monster within—evading, eroding everything I had valued. I believe the only way forward is honesty. It may not be a 'pretty' truth, but it must be heard. I was able to be honest in the doctor's consultation, honest with my manager and honest with those who loved me the most. It didn't cure me, but it was an acceptance of the state that I was in. Maybe because a blood test confirmed this state, it was some kind of validation. I had medical proof of this phase of my life which I never had with post-natal depression, and now I could work on 'fixing' it.

I appreciate that entering this 'non-childbearing' state looks different for everyone. I had decided (we had decided) when our daughter was 4 that we weren't to be parents for a second time. However, there was a completely unexpected wave of 'I want another baby'. Granted, this feeling didn't last long, would have been ludicrous for me at 49 and nigh on impossible with the husband I was firmly committed to. But it still took my breath away. For someone who had never been hugely maternal, this was beyond baffling. Are our gynaecological set-ups so dominant that we feel grief if that choice is taken away from us?

I also feel compelled to hold my hands up to the fact that, like many women, we 'make light' of this episode of our lives. How many times have we been somewhere amongst strangers and declared,

'It's my age…'

'Is it me, or is it hot in here?'

'I can barely remember my own name…'

It is easier to be flippant than deal with the real consequences of this, and it is not bloody funny! I know that I, and those close to me, came dangerously close to 'the end of the road' where they could not contemplate a future that felt like this. Suicide rates in women aged 45-54 have risen by 6% over the past 20 years. Brutal! As with any mental health awareness initiative, there is a stark risk that raising awareness could, in fact, lead to more despair or an inaccurate self or professional diagnosis.

But the other statistic I present to you is that, overall, the suicide rates due to post-natal depression have decreased in recent years, due to increased awareness and support. But the keyword here is support. I have no doubt women in the post-war era suffered just as we have, but did not know what it was and had no name to give it. Then we moved on to women knowing what was wrong, but with nowhere to go from there.

What we need to reach is a point where we have;

*Honest diagnosis with is medically proven, so we don't feel we are losing our minds.

*Equal access to professional support.

* Honesty without flippancy.

*Increased awareness of what this can actually mean to you as a woman.

How can it be okay for half the population to potentially feel as if they have no choices, no options, receiving of zero empathy, simply due to a random throw of the dice which gave them a womb, fallopian tubes and ovaries?

You may have gathered that I am one for taking action—changing things that don't serve me—fixing and facing problems head-on. But this and post-natal depression are the two rollercoaster rides where I had no control. I was strapped in, pushed unwillingly into a dark tunnel, where I couldn't see the end. The brakes were off, and it was, at times, pure terror. No sleep, awaking at midnight for a wee, to be followed by two hours fighting to return to a fitful sleep. An inability to cope with routine life let alone any aspect of conflict or crisis. A weight gain which could never be negated, no matter how much I exercised or followed a diet plan which involved copious amounts of apple cider vinegar or green tea.

But as with all these states of being, there is an end—a better, more insightful state of being. I am no doctor, but HRT worked for me, but not on its own and not straight away. It is also not for everyone. Find what works for you and strive to secure it, and don't give up! There is no right and wrong. I wished (in a similar way to how I planned a holistic labour with a water birth) that I could have handpicked a range of herbs to concoct a remedy that was purely natural—but for me, that was not to be.

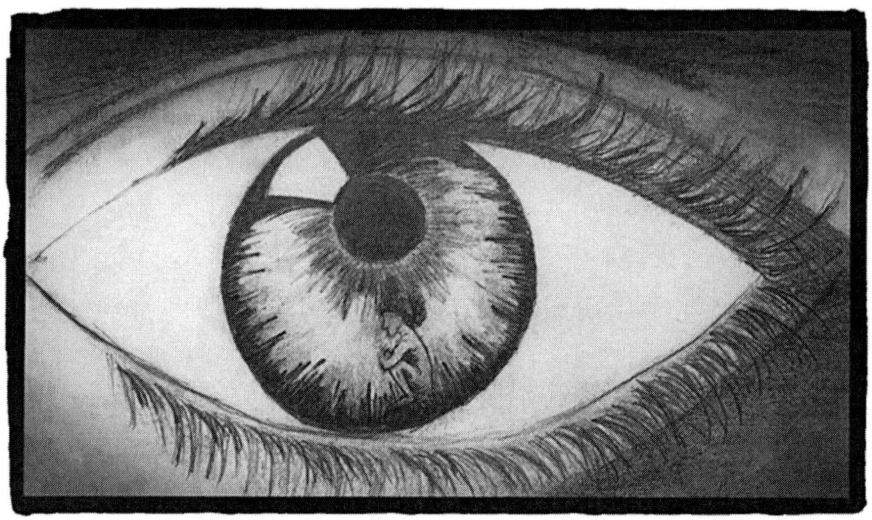

My solution isn't for everyone, but reach out, be honest, and there will be something that will help. Just don't be in denial. God created Eve to be a woman. It is a privilege we carry as much as a burden. It is not our fault, and it will not break us! And when you come out the other side, you will feel empowered, with extra stripes on your wings, to soar into the next phase of womanhood.

Everything Has a Season...

Just as seasons change with predictable reliability without you even noticing it, so do parts of our lives. As a younger woman, my resilience to deal with anything ending was almost non-existent. We are brought up to believe that endings are negative. It has taken a lifetime to realise that an ending is both a potential for a new beginning and a natural part of life.

Long car journeys, asking, ‘Are we nearly there yet?’ is an analogy echoed in so many of our lives. For someone who constantly looks to the end goal, it’s very easy to ignore the rest of the journey. Think what we could see on the way, if we just opened our eyes and didn’t rush.

Maybe it is our culture which leads us to think that the destination has to be our focus. In my case, this is heightened by ADHD, where I have an inbuilt tendency to strive for the highest goal, and if that summit is unattainable, then I wouldn’t even start climbing the mountain. ‘Being in the present’ is a contemporary phrase that may as well have been an encrypted code, an enigma which I never believed was possible.

If only I could have accepted each of those ‘stations’ we stop at on the way. For each ‘station’ can bring its own joys and rewards.

Ending something that is no longer serving us is not always easy and can feel like a failure, an admission of defeat. It is not—it is making a judgment call which can allow space for better things. There are two occasions which have taught me this valuable lesson, and neither came with any kind of warning.

That is not to say, ‘I am a quitter’, I am far from that. In fact, if my beloved soulmate (otherwise known as my dad!) had quit one particular day, I would not be here to tell the story that appears on these pages now. He did, like me, know the point at which something which was not serving him and was just about destruction, should be terminated. Therefore, because of that decision, I am gladly here today.

But this is not Dad's story, even though his influence on my decision-making cannot be denied. My determination not to 'quit' has had to be overridden by my gut instinct to start afresh on two monumental occasions. The endings on both these occasions have been led by my gut instinct, a whispering voice or God, whichever your worldview leads you to decide. But whatever that monkey on my shoulder was called, I wasn't prepared to ignore it. Despite the fact that some of those closest to me either thought I was close to insane or, at best, foolish!

See what you think…

One Friday afternoon, I drove home on high adrenaline to rush back to catch Mum and Dad on their 'Emma-sitting duties'. Dad was one for saying 'we can't stop long', as his fish and chips or Chinese takeaway treat beckoned. It wouldn't be unusual to walk through the door to be greeted by a welcome hug, which soon turned into a goodbye hug to the sound of 'come on, Angela, we'd better be going'. But this day had been just another long slog, at the end of another marathon week, at the end of another tough month. I 'lived' (when I was doing anything **but** living) for the end of the week, but was too exhausted to treasure it. I lived for the end of term, but would break up and invariably be hit by some 'mystery' bug or be too preoccupied to enjoy time off with my family and friends, instead, becoming irritable with an increasingly short fuse, the nearer the end of the holidays came.

Having not been a 'quitter', I had returned to headship after February's 'incident', and whilst I was starting to recover, I knew I was a hamster rattling round its wheel, only just managing to stay upright and occasionally and dramatically falling off. There was no 'lead up' to this decision, other than a somewhat random text earlier that day to an ever-supportive husband to warn him that this was an option and could we carry the financial burden? When I have made my mind up, that is it. Decision done, move on. Mum would often say this was myself and Dad's worst traits.

So, I walked through that door of my home, which never felt like mine because I was never there, to tell Dad to sit down before he got up to say 'farewell'. My memory is not always my strong point, but I clearly remember those words that day.

'I want to be the parent on Emma's playground at the end of the day, rather than the head on a different playground.'

A playground that was often a battleground, and this warrior had had enough. My parental reactions were about as different as they could have been. Now I know they were both from a good place, no judgement on either—but Dad's was one of no questions or hesitations, whilst Mum's was a reminder that I had worked all my life for this and couldn't quit. What I have come to realise, is I had longed all my life for a different state of being, a living in the present which headship would never allow.

The way we all respond to endings is interesting and maybe is connected to some of our attitudes to live for the future or live as if today is our last. The latter has always been my main philosophy! I embarked on headship full of hope, optimism and belief that everyone shared my mindset—of course, they didn't. Ultimately, when I was asked to write my future obituary (on an otherwise forgettable course), I committed to paper what I felt with my heart, and it sure as hell was not to be remembered as only a headteacher.

Therefore, that decision made on a Friday night, followed by a speedily submitted resignation letter written after another weekend where my only thoughts were of school, was led by a need to live my life and protect my precious family.

How can endings driven by love be wrong?

How can endings which lead to healthier, brighter futures be wrong?

How can endings where you have acknowledged your limit and learnt what serves you best…be wrong?

Fast forward eleven years, and I made a carbon copy decision made in very different circumstances.

Stepping off the treadmill in Mum's dying months, I was still that hamster frantically spinning the wheel. I fought a daily battle between being a dutiful daughter and dedicating myself to a career Mum had herself encouraged me to keep a tight hold of. The me – who is a feminist, a defiant only child, a career woman, all fought against the second decision I knew I had to make. Again, I was either led by my inner spirit, whispering voice or God.

That oncologist treating mum, who said not years, not months, but weeks, spoke with knowledge and insight, and at that point, I just knew I had to do the same again and put my family first. The same woman, softening before my very eyes, who once said 'Don't give up work,' was now saying, 'You will be off work, won't you?'

The only place I needed to be was with Mum and back in my safe bubble—my home. This experience was to change my future, but I did not know it. This particular ending was to be the one that led to the words on this page; the rest is yet to unfold, but it is definitely not the end—only the beginning.

SWISS MADE
J.W. BENSON

Safe to Shore

My lighthouse, shining in the darkness, I will follow you. You will carry me safe to shore.

A lifetime of visits to the seaside, noticing the cliffs, the seabirds, smelling the fish and chips, but never quite appreciating this stalwart of a landmark.

Its presence is looming, standing tall and firm, in spite of the eroding cliffs which it protects, crumbling beneath it.

Age does not wither it or stain its pure white veneer. Built to protect, to warn, to alert others, it is unique in its coastal home. A lasting reminder of the past, it has witnessed storms aplenty. It has been privy to disaster: to grief, to fear. But still, it stands resolute, unshaken. So why is it now that I have noticed it?

Maybe because my own life, my landscape, has been filled with darkness since losing my two parents. A light then broke through. I have been led by an invisible force to safety, not always being able to see the potential dangers ahead. When I needed protection, I was steered to a new place.

How often do we keep sailing a boat that is destined to capsize?

Or we desperately try to stay afloat, in waves we know we can't withstand?

I recall a public service advertisement promoting water safety entitled 'Float to Live'. How apt a metaphor this is for our lives! In order for us to be brought safely to shore, for the lighthouse to guide us, we need to stop kicking and fighting and just…float.

When life has forced me to stop, and I have been given time and space, I have then seen the signals this ever-present light was showing me with increased clarity. I allowed myself to be led to a brighter landscape, one where I wouldn't capsize or, even worse, drown.

When life's storms are a torrent, too tumultuous to survive, we need to 'float to live', If we follow the guidance of the light, it is then that we will be brought 'safe to shore'.

Let's Go Fly a Kite!

The secret of genius is to carry the spirit of the child into old age, which means never losing your enthusiasm.

Aldous Huxley

What space do we leave in our adult lives for chances to feel true, unadulterated joy?

Since losing 'them both,' I have had the privilege of more **time**, but I needed to work hard to be in the right headspace to feel **pure joy**. As I romped in the sea off Black Rock Sands in Wales, letting the waves lift me, feeling warmth on my skin, a smile spread over my face which couldn't have been replicated in any other way. A sole figure, watched on by my incredulous husband, I felt free in the most uplifting of ways. Why? Partly because I have loved the sea since being small—it reminds me of Dad and annual jaunts to the coast were repeated for many years when Dad, well in his 70s, would still roll up his trousers and paddle like a 10-year-old.

But more than that, I felt that the spontaneity of the waves, seemingly calm then tumultuous, taking my breath as they enfold, created a feeling that had been lost from my life for a while.

My 9-5 (in reality 7-7) job was perfectly matched to me in many ways, in that the predictability of a timetabled day was 'safe' to me. Equally, you can never fully predict (or would want to) what the children will do or say and almost every day without fail, I would laugh or smile at some unexpected occurrence, like those waves crashing over me on that beach.

Working with children has been a gift, but sadly, the education system (particularly in recent years) does not always allow for much creativity or freedom for children to be children. My fondest memories of the job, looking back, will always be the following:

- End of year visits to the beach for sandcastles, fish and chips and swimming in the sea.
- Residential stays with zip wires, kayaking, card games before bed and PJs.
- Musical productions replicating the likes of Oliver, Joseph, and Bugsy Malone to cheering audiences.
- Cooking adventures (or chaos!) after school, creating smoothies, shortbread and pizzas.

What do you notice? Is it that one Maths lesson that I recall? Is the feedback from the Ofsted inspector? No—the opportunities schools create for joy and wonder will be the ones which endure for a lifetime. I feel so grateful to have worked for Headteachers who allowed me the freedom to be creative and were encouraging of my 'wild and wacky' ideas, which occurred quite regularly. At the start of my career, risk assessments were there, but were not a straitjacket to restrict you. Sadly, I fear for the increasingly restrictive climate that I have left.

If children are not offered chances to feel unbounded joy, what chance do we have as adults?

As a child myself, life lessons were learnt playing out till dusk, no phones, just den making and secret clubs run from the shed. My own parents, even more so. Dad recalled day-long bike rides from Bridlington to Scarborough (surely helmet-less), and Mum recalled playing with her cousins returning home covered in mud (no antibacterial hand gel then!)

With our own daughter, finding a road to live on, where she could play freely with other free spirits, hiding in the woods, splashing in paddling pools and bouncing on trampolines, was a prerequisite to our parenting. Initiatives and societies, such as Scouts and Forest Schools, are tremendous in utilising nature's playground, Sadly, technological advances have tempted children away from some pleasures we sought.

Two of my treasured childhood books were *When We Were Very Young* and *Now We Are Six* by AA Milne. I was fascinated to discover that AA Milne wrote the books for his son, Christopher Robin. But what was meant to entertain and honour his son ended up being a poisoned chalice when Winnie the Pooh and other literary icons from his imagination became all he was known for. AA Milne painted with his words an idyllic picture of what childhood could be. The image of Christopher Robin playing 'Poohsticks' in the quintessentially English setting is etched on my mind, as it will be for many of us. The fact that these creations led to a far from idyllic childhood for his son is sad and ironic. It is another reason why my story could not be told with any honesty until my parents had passed and my daughter was an adult.

Many parents try to shield their children from the grim realities of life, which will come their way soon enough. Not watching the news, holding their toddler's hand down a slide, not letting them cross a road alone are all known examples of this. But do these same parents let their children have a phone, be open to all that social media lures them towards and far earlier than is needed or healthy?

Shocked does not adequately describe my reaction when discovering that the latest statistics show 1 in 5 children aged 3-4 have a phone. What kind of society are we living in where this is in any way acceptable or justifiable? The world AA Milne (and Enid Blyton) created of stone skimming, adventures in the woods, and midnight feasts may be somewhat sanitised and idealistically unachievable in the twenty-first century. But it is these adventures, ones led by nature and not technology, which will burn long in our memories, not playing on a phone or watching a YouTube clip.

So, if we are to 'carry the spirit of the child into old age' as I did when I jumped the waves, we need to make sure our children still have the chance to experience pure, unbounded joy where they laugh until it hurts, blow bubbles watching where they land and make daisy chains until the sun sets.

As adults, many of us scarred by life and trauma, we also need to leave space for joy and peace to enter. For some, it may be riding a bike, climbing a mountain or for me, braving the cold water. Even when our biological clocks are begging us to slow down, it doesn't have to mean less joy, less laughter. I have laughed more in recent months when unburdened by a school timetable and caring duties. I eventually now feel like that wide-eyed girl on the front page. It can be so much fun to embrace your inner child, and we must never let it fade!

Deeply Rooted

Living in Nottinghamshire, local folklore was part of my upbringing when visiting the Major Oak, the place where Robin Hood was reputed to have taken shelter. Visits here as a toddler standing at its base were the equivalent of an ant gazing up at a giraffe. This beast of a tree has been steeped in history, but it needed modern interventions to protect it from decline. In the same year as I was born, fences were erected to protect this precious entity from root damage.

Less aged in terms of years, but equally impressive and symbolic is the Sycamore Gap tree, which ironically is named by some as the Robin Hood Tree. Not due to any allegiance to this green, feathered superhero in his cap, but due to its stunning panorama being used in a scene of the 1991 film.

The positioning of this tree in a glacial dip meant it became an iconic sight, revered by many…until the day two soulless individuals decided (for reasons only known to them) that they would fell it down, for a laugh, a dare or something equally irrelevant. The shockwaves of this action rippled through the whole country, and many tears were shed over this arboreal murder.

Trees are steeped in symbolism and significance, depending on their species or culture. Evergreen trees speak for themselves in representing immortality, keeping a tight hold on their leaves all year round. Sadly, that wasn't the case for our Sycamore Gap. The aforementioned oak trees represent strength and power shown by their immense stature. The beech trees that overlook our family home and the first sight I wake to every morning, are associated with femininity—I quite happily take that as something to surround myself with!

Widely used within books, marketing, and branding is the Tree of Knowledge. Having worked in five schools over my career, four out of the five use a tree as an integral part of their school logo, along with thousands of schools across the country. Why? The Tree of knowledge symbolises growth (which we would wish for our children), knowledge (for which it is our job to exude) and a link with nature (to encourage today's children to be tomorrow's protectors of the planet).

One of my schools created a tree of knowledge out of recycled bottle tops during the years of COVID-19 school disturbance. It was hung with pride in the school garden—representing our place of learning as well as our desire to protect the environment.

The fact that trees derive from something so small but can live for thousands of years if protected and respected is a true wonder of nature. As humans, we also need fences built around us to protect us from time to time. We also, like our tree ancestors, grow in stages, at times a little unruly, in need of a clip, but constantly renewing through the seasons. It is the people and places which ground us and keep our roots firm which secure our greatest growth.

You will all have your 'go-tos' when needing grounding: a journey back to the family home, a stay at a yoga retreat, reunions with childhood friends or a strong belief system or faith. These allow us to remain steadfast and not get carried away. We can all recall 'stars' who succumb to the lure of fame, and their lives can be cut short way too soon. The difference with celebrities who acquire longevity is that they will often state that they have remained 'grounded'.

The dictionary definition of 'grounded' is 'well-balanced and sensible'. I profess to not always being either of these things, but I do know I benefit from loved ones who will act on my behalf, in the 'common sense department'!

The other element of a tree's identity is its unique way of showing its age: dendrochronology. To you and me: counting the rings of its cross-section of the trunk. This is not only 'mind-blowing' that Mother Nature can represent the passing of time in such an intrinsic way, but also how beautiful these concentric rings are proudly shown as a badge of maturity. How do we show our rings of maturity? Every line, wrinkle, blemish, scar is part of our story. Some of us feel we can wear these with pride, some hide them in shame. Just as that attack was made on the Sycamore Gap, attacks are made on us. For some, these are physical, for some spiritual, but for all of us…life's journey will throw turmoil upon us. Every experience will be etched upon us, whether we choose to hide the lines or spend a fortune correcting them with the latest laser, Botox or surgical procedure. Visibly, the tree can be trimmed or brutally felled, but its history and life will live on.

The outrage the nation felt when the Sycamore Gap was attacked, moved onto a determination to make something positive come out of a devastating act of brutality. The National Trust were instrumental in the 49 'Trees of Hope' saplings, awarded to charitable or educational establishments to nurture. This will ensure that, whilst the original tree will always be missing from the landscape near Hadrian's Wall, 49 other 'descendants' of this legendary tree will become things of beauty for even more people to appreciate and treasure. The 15 National Parks our country is incredibly fortunate to call our own will also receive saplings along with several sites near Hadrian's Wall. How apt that in the same way many of us return home in times of turmoil, the Sycamore Gap will be doing the same?

With myself and others that I know, Art and creativity can be used as an act of healing after trauma. An artist, Charlie Winney, retained part of this special tree to form an integral part of his sculpture. It also features carefully chosen words on curved, steam-bent wood. The idea being that as you explore the art installation, in different directions, it allows you to take words such as 'old', 'friend', 'glad', 'strong', 'lost', etc., to create a poem personal to you. Benches also allow visitors to sit and ponder, and the trunk is free to be 'hugged'. What a remarkable story of humans restoring nature this is, and how refreshing that this tree will longer far linger in all our memories than the two criminals imprisoned and whose names we will soon forget.

Trees have always had a greater significance in my life than I realised. On the evening my dad drove home, Mum and myself in hospital I cannot imagine the feelings that were flooding through him. But the fact that he paused his journey to take a photograph of a tree that caught his eye, stood against the sunset on the day he became my dad is hugely significant. He then referred to this 26 years later on my wedding day in his emotion-packed speech when he said, "Just as that tree still stands strong, so does Joanna grow in confidence and stature." It was at that point that his voice quivered with tears.

Trees are also enormously significant in the Bible. Genesis states that God's hands create plants soon after he forms Adam and then places him under the tree. The text of Genesis acknowledges that trees 'keep humans alive', 'prepare shelter' and 'food for life'. In that first garden stood two trees: The 'tree of life' (also termed 'the tree of souls') and the 'tree of knowledge'. The latter is renowned for providing the fruit of temptation, devoured by Adam and Eve, leading them and a nation into a world of sin and death. Maybe this first event of the Bible has more similarities to the Sycamore Gap incident than we thought?

But I leave this reflection returning to this school symbol with the Tree of knowledge, a symbol of wisdom. If God intended this tree to give us a chance to exercise moral culpability and make the 'right' choice, then we can see why it is used on so many school logos. Our children will be faced throughout their lives with choices, moral dilemmas and if, as educators/ parents, we can provide firm roots, the hope is that they will stand firm.

I can honestly say that in 29 years, never as a teacher have I been given an apple! However, this phrase apparently originated in the nineteenth century when, in rural communities, children wanting to show appreciation to the teacher would give the most readily available produce, an apple. I may have never been given an apple (not sure I would have wanted one plonked on my desk), but I know that the thanks and gratitude many of us receive as teachers will be treasured and held in our hearts, and hopefully, those seeds of wisdom we hope to have passed on to them will forever inspire them also.

Postcards from My Hometown

Robin Hood, the Emmet Clock, Rock City, the home of Lace, Raleigh Bikes and DH Lawrence. What do the following things have in common?

The heart of the East Midlands and my hometown of Nottingham.

Our towns of our birth, where we first were allowed off the leash on our own, shape us in a way we don't always realise until later in life.

These are my postcards from my hometown…

I begin with DH Lawrence. Living just a mile or so from his birthplace and immersed in the countryside, which provided the settings for his iconic writing and having ancestors who were miners, it was somewhat of a given that I would come into contact with his writing quite early on in my reading career. He writes of my hometown being…*an extremely beautiful countryside, just between the red sandstone and oak trees of Nottingham…the mines were, in a sense, an accident in the landscape. (1929)*

As I return to the familiar villages of Brinsley and Eastwood to this day, the coal mines may be long gone, but the red sandstone and oak trees remain. Within the toil and grit of a mining community the fact that Lawrence was able to introduce such raw passion and romance through his writing, whilst retaining honesty about both the beauty and brutality of our hometown leaves him as one of our most prolific writers. The fact that 'Lady Chatterley's Lover' was banned in 1960 for explicitness and obscenity seems incredulous now in our current society, where our boundaries have widened so much, and the written word is sometimes neglected in preference for online forums, displaying surely far worse than an illicit love affair between a lady and the 'helping hand'. Lawrence was undoubtedly an interesting character, but his romanticism shaped me as a teenage reader. I also felt an affinity with him, as his father and uncle worked at Brinsley colliery (which he names 'Minton Pit').

My long walks with Dad would pass by the majestic headstocks, still standing until recently snatched away, due to health and safety concerns. Again, how ironic that men died in the pit, but in our risk-averse society, we cannot leave a mark of our past standing for fear it will collapse! These headstocks were a reminder of what this area had to endure when the mines were closed during the Thatcher reign in the 1980s. The mines may long be gone, but the ethos and mindset didn't fade. To return to Brinsley and Mum's closest neighbours, it is as if nothing has changed since those days of Lawrence, whilst you know that absolutely everything has.

My second postcard begins with the words from another Nottinghamshire writer, Lord Byron, with his words;

She walks in beauty, like the night
Of cloudless chimes and starry skies;
And all that's best of dark and bright
Meet in her aspect and her eyes… **(Lord Byron)**

I have no idea who Lord Byron was referring to, but I am using his words of poetry to refer to a mechanical beauty, which was a renowned and revered meeting place for Nottingham residents for decades and is the next postcard I send to you.

The Emmet Clock was the jewel in Nottingham's crown for many years. It found its spiritual home in 1973, the year before I was born and after a brief break away to be restored with its future in doubt, it made its journey back home in 2015. It stands proud once more to be admired by a new generation. This mechanical dancing wonder is adorned with butterflies, rotating squirrels and birds, with water flowing over copper petals and represents everything nature gives us. It creates awe and wonder in anyone casting their eyes upon it for the first time.

The addition of music to serenade the 'show' every 15 minutes adds to the drama. Seats positioned at the base allow onlookers, such as myself and mum for years every single Saturday, to 'people watch'. It invites you to experience the peace of a garden within a busy metropolis of a shopping centre. The wishing well adds to the air of mystery and superstition, as coins are thrown into this northern 'Trevi Foundation'. This manmade thing of beauty every week of my childhood was also a place of safety (who could lose me at this place where we had arranged to meet?) and a lesson that nature is forever giving in its works of art.

Sometimes the brain and creativity of a human director are needed to take the wonders of nature to a different audience. Within an industrial, urban setting, what an inspiration it is to have butterflies, jewels, and squirrels dancing to classical music? For many years, the Emmet Clock sang and danced to all who passed before her, and I would use the words of Byron to say that this was a place where 'all that's best of dark and bright meet in her aspect and her eyes'.

From 'people watching' as a child, experiencing the thrill of going home with shopping bags aplenty, to a feisty 17-year-old who had itchy feet and yearned to experience the 'life' within the city and all that it had to offer, a naïve village girl who wanted to 'live'. Therefore, we must now move from the poetry of Lawrence and the magical clockwork of Emmet to the far less refined…'Rock City!'

A dark, heaving stew pot of smells, noise and vibration was my regular Thursday night at a certain Rock City. The benchmark of every week for this teenager, seeking freedom, seeking excitement, seeking life! Doc Martens donned, sticking to the floor, ready to dance. But is it dance as we know it? Wedged between strangers, sardines in a can, no room to breathe, let alone dance. As *Smells Like Teen Spirit* booms with a predictable regularity, heads are spinning, rocketing from side to side, forward and back, aiming for oblivion. A yearning to get completely lost in this place.

Time seems to stand still, yet speed towards that fateful point in the night where the taxi calls or the lights rudely halt this melting pot of youth, Cinderella like. The acidic stench, almost toxic, surrounds us as we ironically 'dance' to this anthemic Nirvana track. How many feet have trodden this dance floor? How many pints have been spilt? How many nights won or lost in this mecca?

Fast forward some 30-plus years, and four friends head to the same venue, but with eyes wide open, minus the Doc Martens and at the unusually early time of 3 pm! These four strong, independent women have become swamped at times by life and responsibility, but for a few short hours, all **that** can be put aside, just as worries were put aside on that sticky dance floor in 1990. Stood in the queue, expectant…chats are heard about mundane Saturday morning rituals such as putting the washing on or a casserole in the oven. In the days of nearing 50, we seem only able to justify three hours of dancing and drinking by stating how many household jobs we've done prior to this temporary slot of freedom!

This new 'movement' of like-minded souls comes under the umbrella of 'Day Fever'—sweeping the nation to mop up the pressures of middle age, transporting us back to our carefree youth! It started in my home town and has become somewhat of a phenomenon. Long may our 19-year-old selves be able to boogie the night…sorry, afternoon away!

Finally, my last postcard has to be the sacred City Ground, home of Nottingham Forest. Dad's passion for all sports, but particularly football, soon became something I shared as a teenager. Not for playing the game, sadly, but as a spectator. You can imagine his immense pride and joy when his granddaughter went on to lace up her own football boots years later, relishing the opportunity to watch her at any available chance. But it is the times, he and I visited the home of 'the reds' to cheer on the likes of Stuart Pearce, Nigel Clough, Des Walker and (my adored) Nigel Jemson! In all honesty, it was probably as a 17-year-old, less about the offside rule and more about the 'poster boys'. But I am proud to admit that yes… I can explain the offside rule!

The whole experience began from the walk to the ground, surrounded by strangers simultaneously marching towards a victorious afternoon. And continued with the half-time refreshments (to this day, the fact that a pie is traditional football fare, baffles me), but when in Rome, and all that! The anticipation and camaraderie shared when you attend a home match is a feeling that is quite priceless and one which I am grateful Dad shared with me, and a legacy I was only too keen to pass on to my daughter.

This postcard so far could be true of any football ground, but the City Ground will not only always have a special place in my heart, but in footballing history. Its unique location alongside the River Trent and nestling between the now affluent West Bridgford and the less 'des-ress' of the Meadows, is intriguing and somehow represents the melting pot and juxtaposition of Nottingham. For me, having lived here, it can show the best of urban regeneration and the worst of neglected suburbs, such as the Meadows.

The City Ground is also unusual in being shadowed by two other iconic sporting arenas: Meadow Lane—the home of rivals Notts County and the impressive cricketing palace of Trent Bridge. So, when visiting this area, chances are, whoever you meet will be a fan of one of these teams. If not, why not? One of the lasting highlights of my footballing ventures with my dad was when, following their defeat in the 1991 FA Cup final, we welcomed this revered team back home, along with thousands of others. The sea of red and white paraphernalia surrounded these local heroes as they stood aboard the open-top bus. There is nothing quite like the feeling when celebrating success (even though this team had been defeated in the final), with a footballing 'family'.

I return to the same sentiments I shared in the chapter 'Celebrate the failures'. The way we respond to defeat is as crucial as the way we respond to success, and nowhere is that more visible than with football supporters. There is nothing 'supportive' about 'supporters' who leave a stadium before the final whistle, simply because their team aren't winning. But that certainly was not the sentiment on that glorious day in Nottingham in 1991.

And finally, I conclude this chapter with a nod to another Nottinghamshire author, whose story left a lasting impact on me recently. Jacob Dunne's remarkable route to redemption is reminiscent of the aforementioned Nicky Cruz. Growing up in Nottingham, specifically the Meadows, he acted impulsively but irreversibly one night in a city pub, with an act that changed his life forever and took another. This was only the beginning of the story; the rest I would strongly urge you to read. He now uses his experience to educate others with the aim of preventing anyone from taking this route to oblivion. His book 'Right from Wrong' and the play his story became, 'Punch' are the most powerful, wonderfully inspiring pieces of literature I have encountered in recent years.

So, from legends like Robin Hood to footballing icons, from poets like Lawrence and Byron to contemporary public speakers such as Jacob Dunne, and from iconic meeting places around the Emmet clock to the dark buzz of Rock City—there is much to shout about in my hometown, which runs through my blood. Red, of course!

Each Length Swam, A Renewal of My Spirit

When signing up to a charity swim for the incredibly worthy cause, Macmillan Cancer, little did I know what an undertaking this was to be. For a serial fundraiser who signs up for such things after a crisis, or initiates such activities within my school settings, this was just another one to tick off my list. No bother at all to set up the 'Just Giving' page and spread the word by the power of social media.

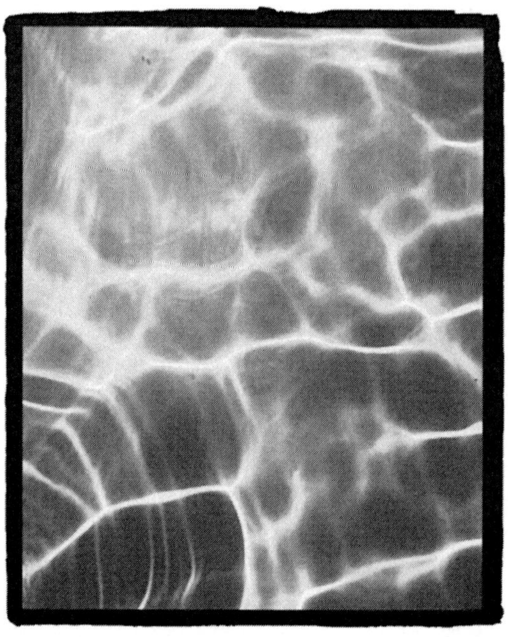

Given that Mum had 'instructed' me to 'get fit' in her last few days, I thought this would fit the bill perfectly.

Prior to this, my recollections of swimming were not particularly positive ones. I am a self-taught amateur, after horrendous 70s, 80s school lessons where the segregation of non-swimmers meant a shallow pool, being dismissively given a float and being left to flounder like a proverbial hippo! Never mind the indignity of communal changing rooms, a journey on a jalopy of a bus and a return to school for the weekly times table test. There was no wonder I dreaded Fridays from the ages of 7-11!

Luckily, I had a friend who could swim better than I and we 'enjoyed' weekly trips to a slightly more salubrious pool, where laughter was more likely to be on the cards, and a bag of chips was our reward on the way home. So, it wasn't all bad, but I was far from a confident swimmer. It was a source of constant amusement that my dad grew up by the sea, in his 'happy place', but whilst he was keen to roll his shorts up and paddle, his feet were never to leave that shingle base!

In stark contrast, having paid for and accompanied my daughter to numerous swimming lessons, I acknowledge that my generation was certainly the 'head above water, breaststroke swimmers' who ploughed on, whilst more proficient, dolphin-like creatures glided past us with grace and speed. I had always been in 'awe' of this skill, one that my daughter possesses (at the cost of thousands of pounds in lessons, no doubt), but very rarely uses that skill now.

On the first day of the challenge, my commitment to this swim began. I have also recently fallen in love with cold-water swimming, so it was my initial intention to complete this challenge in predominantly cold water; however, the good old British weather put paid to this in the first week of June. I was to experience something I hadn't expected when swimming in the familiar local indoor pool. A monumental flashback…to when I was 30, a new Mum trying to navigate all that this entailed, as well as returning to teaching.

It was 2004, and I finished my working week on Wednesday lunchtime and literally 'forced' myself to go to the pool—exhausted beyond compare —to swim 40 long and repetitive lengths. If you had known me at the time, you would be the first to acknowledge that I was hardly at the peak of my physical fitness. That may be the 'understatement' of this century!

Looking back, it was a somewhat desperate attempt to feel free and do something just for me—at a time when all freedom appeared to be lost. Did I gain anything from this regular Wednesday ritual? I very much doubt it. I recall that some weeks, the chlorine-filled water disguised the tears which streamed down my face. I can look back at this now with a retrospective glance at how this experience, horrific at the time, shaped me.

My metaphorical affair with cold immersion started with a programme featuring Wim Hof. Now, I like to aim high, but I will not be breaking any records in Arctic conditions, but my request for a birthday present of a cold pod was initially smirked at. Another health fad, something to gather dust in the garage? But my ever-supportive husband obliged and the daily morning ritual began. (Boy was I determined to prove him wrong!)

Research provides scientific explanations as to why this works, but for me, it is far less complex. I have to sit still, I have to breathe, I have to endure at least 5 minutes, and for someone with ADHD, that is not a common ingredient in my life. It is a ritual I dare not break, for fear it will lead to a day where depression sneaks in as a response to grief. Therefore, every morning I take the plunge.

My response to being out of control after the birth of my daughter and the death of my Mum 21 years later is to focus on something positive that I can achieve, but that challenges me. But I swim each length now with purpose, but also reflection. There are no tears this time around, instead…I count! Counting up, counting down, even counting in batches of 10, but nothing more enters my head.

Given my overactive, battery-driven brain, I have no choice but to 'switch off'. Something I have been told to do all my life, but never managed—not even in sleep. It is a surprise that I can do this, but the concentration needed to find the right pace, rhythm and stroke technique is all my menopausal brain can manage.

If I rush, I'll tire.

If I stop, I won't restart.

If I think, I'll go under. (What a metaphor this is!) So, all I can do is swim. Still not 'dolphin-like' but with more of a sense of calm than I thought was possible.

Water has always had the power to not only cleanse but heal—just ask intrepid travellers or pilgrims to the River Ganges or the Dead Sea! (You can tell my Mum was an RE teacher!). Having been raised in the Christian faith, I know only too well the significance of a baptism in water. In this transitional period of my life, living with grief, a time leaving behind a lifetime's profession, a time for new opportunities—each length swam is…*truly a renewal of the spirit.*

Through the Looking Glass

The human attitude to mirrors is diverse and fascinating. In a similar way to the way a camera is supposed to depict an accurate snapshot, the view in a mirror can vary dramatically. This can depend on our emotions at that minute, our self-esteem (or lack of it) and the actual mirror. It is surely not an urban myth that mirrors in changing rooms are invariably set up to flatter, whereas on the way out of my gym, the ridiculously oversized mirrors add at least two stone to the image they reflect. This leaves you feeling deflated but equally determined to return to the gym the next day.

Add to these common distortions the fairground attraction of the 'Hall of Mirrors', which is devised to entertain, and there is no wonder our perceptions of ourselves can be warped. I mean, it is brutal!

I know I am not alone in avoiding mirrors at certain points in my life, in the same way that I would avoid photographs being taken. Even on my lowest of days, I would refrain from leaving the house for the fear of catching a glance of myself in a shop window, which would wound me so intensely that I would feel mortified and ashamed. It is part of the reason I seek solace in a swimming pool, as even though the water appears 'mirror-like', it disguises everything wobbling about under the surface, and everyone appears equal from the perspective of the onlooker.

We cannot simply blame mirrors alone for our insecurities regarding our appearances. Having been a 'normal' sized child, a 'skinny' teenager, an 'obese' new mother, a 'toned, athletic' 35-year-old, an 'obese' tired professional nearing 40, a 'toned, athletic' 45-year-old, then a woman processing a double-whammy of grief, who returned to 'obese' status. Do the words 'yo-yo' come to mind?

Of course, some people's weight 'classifications' (apologies for the terminology, which in itself I loathe) do not fluctuate as much as mine have, but I don't happen to know anyone who would admit to being truly happy in their skin. For me, my self-esteem issues were not at all simple.

Personality-wise, I have rarely lacked confidence and feel comfortable in most social situations—a high achiever, borderline extrovert who likes to entertain. I recently wrote when comparing myself to a flower, 'I would be a carnation, a little jagged round the edges, but whose beauty comes into its own when cut and can bring joy to a room'.

Sadly, this confident façade can sometimes hide a woman who is not always comfortable in the clothes that she wears, the size that she is or what the mirror is showing. I have always been very vulnerable to the opinions of others and freely admit I seek assurance – a classic 'people pleaser'. Being an only child, comparisons cannot be made from within the family, and as a child, I always knew I was loved unconditionally.

Living with one parent who was incredibly demonstrative and complementary saw me through times when I felt as far away from beautiful as possible. Even at times when others were 'attacking' me, the minute I came back to the safe cocoon of home, I knew how precious I was, and it restored me. This is why, having lost my dad, I craved assurance and praise I always received from him, but it was not always forthcoming. The more I had to go without it, the more I craved it. I can only liken this to the endless diets I have been on, where a banned food became all I could think about.

An inherent overthinker, I read more into what people **don't** say, more than what they do. This is heightened if someone dared to tell me not to wear a certain outfit because it wasn't flattering. Yes, this often happened! I cannot comprehend why someone who loves you would deem it appropriate to say 'don't wear that'. But they did, and these remarks can sadly be the ones you hold onto and remember for far longer than you would wish. With the children I have taught and the one I have raised, I have endeavoured to use praise to bolster self-confidence. I look to see the spark of brilliance in everyone, however well-hidden that spark might be and I put in regular effort to make it shine.

Maybe when we hear critical voices, we are hearing the speaker's issues with self-esteem, not ours. The classic reason behind bullying behaviours is often jealousy and covering their own feelings of insignificance with a blanket of attack and criticism.

It has taken several stages, not a 'weight-loss journey' but what I now call 'weight acceptance journey', to lead me to a point where I care far less about others' external views of me. I have learnt that what looks back at me from the mirror is a strong, confident woman whose lumps and bumps do not define her.

This is not to say that I do not strive to be the 'toned and athletic' 55-year-old (as I attained this at 35, 45, and I like a challenge!). I now aim not to give those gym mirrors the satisfaction! If I don't like what I see, who else is going to? I have been very blessed with friends in later life and (luckily a husband) who affirm me and are not scared to tell me they love and value me. I have learnt that I was previously somewhat of a 'magnet', attracting those who would drain my self-esteem, in order to bolster their own. No more.

Mirrors shouldn't be feared, as they help us face facts. But only we can control our response to them. Who knows, on my next visit to the seaside, I may even enter that 'hall of mirrors' for once?

It Was Never About the Food...

Please take note that this episode is not mine. It is told of someone very special to me who showed immense bravery in her recovery, as well as sharing her story with me and now with you.

Growing up as a keen 'foodie', she once stated that the only food she wouldn't eat was pesto! A social eater, meals out with friends and family were an essential part of life. This was never predicted, never 'on the cards', until a combination of two elements led to a spiral of self-doubt. The influence that our peer group can have on us is immense. As with my own journey, you can easily slide from 'part of the popular crowd' where you are known and valued for your quirkiness and natural beauty, to being plunged into a new environment where, keen to fit in, you start to make comparisons with others.

In a world of filters, instant 'snaps' on social media and live streams, inaccurate judgements can be made on our appearances, leaving us feeling we need to conform to a 'norm'. But whose 'norm'? I am telling her story, because a book written in 2025, without a section dedicated to a recovery from addiction and which didn't address the pressure enforced on our young adults, would be a story only half told.

This confident, sociable young woman found herself in a circle of 'gorgeous' girls, where current society's expectations did not embrace curly hair, when everyone's was straight. Did not embrace a bubbly personality when others were silent faces on a screen. Did not embrace someone who spoke her truth, when everyone else was happy to 'shut up' and quieten their voice. No blame is to be attached to the girls who fall into this gaping hole of conformity, but if it is not you, it can lead to deteriorating self-esteem, where you feel you will never live up to expectations.

The greatest misconception regarding this journey is that it is about food and losing weight. About vanity. It is not. As with any mental illness, there is rarely one moment of crisis; it is a gradual decline, like a dark stranger creeping into your safe space, moving in and then completely taking over.

I said that there were two elements contributing to this decline, and the second was monumental for all of us. It was called the COVID pandemic. When the world shut down, our gates were locked, our diaries were erased, and our choices were massacred! So, when found in a circle of friends, which probably wasn't serving her, there was no option but to retain these associations online, intensifying the problem that already existed. We can never underestimate the impact that this period of 'weirdness' had on our society. I am not here to assess whether it was worse for school-aged children, young adults or our elders, but all we can speak is our truth, and this was very real.

As more weight was lost and the calories were obsessively counted, it was understandable to think this constituted making a healthy choice to be fit and slender during this enforced period of confinement. How many of us bought exercise equipment, watched online Pilates classes, cooked healthily for the first time (remember banana bread) and started running? When all stimulation and human interaction are snatched away from us, we look to find anything which can motivate us, give us a reason to get up in the morning and try to achieve something positive from this hell we are all faced with. As our circles became smaller, our issues intensified, and it was not long before the beast that is 'anorexia' was very visible for everyone to see.

This is where an eating disorder can differ from other mental illnesses, such as post-natal depression or anxiety, because everyone can see your decline. Your physical figure can become something you don't recognise as you. Loved ones can see something that you might not yet have acknowledged. Those who have known you since birth are questioning how this has happened to someone who was previously so 'alive', so 'full of energy'. This Duracell bunny's batteries had certainly run out. At this point, both physically and mentally, there was nothing left in her tank. Waking up every morning, famished with hunger, but knowing she **couldn't** eat.

Allowing herself a salad for lunch, but overcompensating with extreme exercise, exerting her body to complete something that it wasn't fuelled for. The daily routine of counting calories became a destructive obsession, which was utterly exhausting. The debate over whether all menus in restaurants should list nutritional information is complex. From an awareness and allergy perspective, clearly it is required, but to have no choice but to see those numbers in front of you may not always be beneficial. Those recovering from an eating disorder do not need this constant reminder of a habit they need to break. Counting calories can be an effective strategy for some, but it can also lead you down the route of feeling highly destructive food related guilt.

The other thing to consider is our approaches to eating disorders as onlookers. How do we approach those we love when they are at their 'rock bottom'? We can say 'you aren't right' and the listener will not listen. We can ignore it and back away, distancing ourselves from something we are not emotionally equipped for. We have all lost friends who are 'fair-weather' friends, not ready to survive the harsh winters. When we are recovered enough to look back, we can see how others may have viewed our actions as 'selfish'.

But this was not our intention. We didn't mean this to happen. It was never about 'not eating', and for that reason, our loved ones are completely justified in saying 'please love, just eat!' If only life were that simple! Why should any of us feel guilt for something we didn't actively choose? I have been there, not related to eating, but when in recovery, the guilt can consume us and delay our journey to wellness. When we look back from a place of strength, it is right that we see that the scales of guilt should not be placed on our shoulders to drag us down.

Therefore, recovery is only possible with an acceptance of what has happened. What makes any of us hold on when all we want to do is let go? When at 'rock bottom', many of us will choose to live—no matter how hard that is to do—for the sake of our loved ones beside us. Having a healthy support network is crucial in any mental health recovery. That is not to say that without this, you are doomed. But for myself and our brave fighter stuck in a quagmire of self-doubt, self-sabotage and sheer hunger, the presence of loved ones was key.

As relatives are required to provide this warm blanket of safety, it can be very challenging to know how to react, what to say and what not to say. Some relatives may avoid the issue, either because they simply find it too hard to approach or fear saying the wrong thing and making the situation worse. In some cases, we believe it will go away if we ignore it. There is no judgment on this understandable reaction, but it can be a mismatch with what the one suffering requires or needs.

Honest dialogue and acceptance, seeking medical intervention at the right time, were imperative in this particular recovery journey. Finding professional help which is multi-layered can be a roll of the dice, another cruel case of the postcode lottery.

Within days of facing hospitalisation (a prospect none of us wish to throw 'what ifs?' at), a triple package of therapy was instigated as part of a medical trial. The chance of this arising was minute, but incredibly fortuitous. Three sessions of therapy a week, however, was to a certain degree 'overkill' and draining. Whilst the approaches and aspects of this therapy differed, and all may have played a part in this recovery jigsaw, on reflection, it was 'too much'. Most mental health practitioners will state that some therapy is far more effective later down the line. When in the midst of hell, we cannot always breathe deeply enough to enable talking therapies to take hold. Too deep are we in darkness; glimmers of light may break through, but we are far from ready to open our eyes to enlightenment.

Within the midst of a crisis, a 'simple' choice can be the turning point. Looking ahead (with blind hope) to a university place waiting for her, she knew it was an equation of eat, and you stand a chance of being able to access your dreams of travelling, followed by embarking on a university course. Don't eat, and this will definitely not happen. She was on a rollercoaster, out of control, but knew she wanted to stop, knew she **had** to eat, one mouthful at a time.

Each pound gained brought her closer to 'permission' to travel. No magic wand was waved, in that the delights of pasta, pizza and prosecco were tolerated. Not relished, as they would be today. However, it was a signal that she could not only survive but live, and this spurred her on to the bright lights of Salford—namely Media City! A last-minute decision is often made from the heart rather than the head. My experience shows that I can certainly vouch for this! Choosing a media degree rather than one which would have led to a life in the theatre, surrounded by competition, auditions, potential disappointment and judgments made on looks, proved to be the last piece in the recovery jigsaw.

As she embarked on hosting radio shows, this was the perfect choice of direction, which meant judgments would only be made on her voice and personality, not on her body shape. We all seek approval and affirmation—wanting to know we are all liked is natural. Therefore, rising figures and positive interactions from her 'Blabber Mouth' radio show were all she needed. As was her new social circle. For the first time in a while, she 'found her people'. A potential career in journalism was not in her 'plan' years back, but it would turn out to be her saviour.

We need to find our true vocations, ones which suit our skill sets, but also suit our personalities and psyches. I joke that I, too, had a childhood dream to be a theatre performer, entertaining audiences who respond with standing ovations. Of course, I know that my ADHD meaning I need routine and structure, along with a reluctance to live out of a suitcase, would have meant that childhood dream would have actually been my nightmare (apart from the fact that I can't sing and neither can I dance!) How many career advisors at school ask us to consider our personalities as much as our qualifications?

Only later in life have I acknowledged that whilst I was a committed teacher who achieved milestone after milestone, the early, chaotic starts with stressful drives to work, were not conducive to my personality. We need to follow our hearts and listen to ourselves when choosing vocations, and of course, nothing is for life. But only we know ourselves best.

We return to Salford and the fact that the same social media channels which contributed to her decline as a teenager were now being utilised in a much more positive way. Her passion to help others drove her to reach out to an unknown audience with brutal honesty about what she had experienced and the lessons she had learnt. How many of us would want to hide our darkest times, push them back into our distant memories? But for me, true recovery comes with acceptance and allowing others to share aspects of your story, with the aim of finding hope in your survival.

As with therapy, this cannot be achieved straight away. No pressure should be placed on speeding along your recovery; it takes far more time than our impatient selves would wish. For many, an eating disorder can improve and then re-emerge as an even larger monster than before. The proportion of sufferers who relapse is significant. The first question I asked her was, 'Do you feel fully recovered?' and this was perhaps unfair. I doubt any of us feel 'fully recovered' from anything we have experienced. Her response was far more insightful than the question I asked. She now feels compelled to not only share her story but to 'be who she really is'.

To live her life fully and authentically, not shying away from that curly hair, an 'out there' personality and seeking only relationships which will embrace that. If we believe recovery is about us changing **who** we are, we are misled. It may well be about changing **where** we are or the way we spend our days, but primarily, it is about accepting ourselves first and then surrounding ourselves with those who see our true beauty.

I dedicate this episode to the incredible woman it is about, and know this experience of how she stitched herself back together is part of the wonderful fabric of her life. I know she will go on to use her media influence to share her experience and energy with a whole new generation.

Grief Is the Price We Pay for Love

This insightful quote has been uttered to me many times over the years. It comes from the mouth of the late Queen Elizabeth II as her response to the 9/11 tragedy. I appreciate the sentiment and that it is intended with love, but for me, it doesn't quite sit right. At some points in my grief, I have almost found it patronising. For me, it suggests that I, in some way, 'deserve' the loss and pain of grief. The passionate love I have felt for my parents, my godmother, my job and my 'not to be baby', does not mean that I deserve this severity of pain. If we venture down the line of 'deserving grief', then we start to evoke guilt.

Guilt is my default emotion. My striving for perfection has meant that, in some way, I have always fallen short. I believe that no one benefits from me thrashing myself with a whip! Being released from guilt is truly liberating. This does not give us freedom to run amok and treat people badly or be flippant about the decisions and choices we make. But I do have to trust that by the age of 51, I have a strong enough moral compass to rely on myself to act in a reasonable, compassionate way.

Guilt was so often felt about seemingly trivial things. Why don't you try listing what **you** feel guilty about and weigh up what will really happen as a result of your actions? Will there be lasting repercussions? Probably not.

- I would feel guilt (expressed in phone calls to Mum) when I had rung in sick to work. I was always genuinely ill, of course, but any teacher will know that the guilt at what our class will be doing in our absence leads us to worry so much, that we do not don't really recover, rest or recuperate. It is crippling. Guilt led me to work on an iPad from my hospital bed! Really!
- I would feel guilt for choosing a cake with my coffee or having toast instead of a yoghurt for breakfast. Various slimming initiatives do not

feed our bodies but 'feed' our constant guilt. When you reach weigh-in day and step on 'the scales of shame', it can be a self-deprecating cycle that works on guilt alone and is highly damaging. Yes, I appreciate the need to be healthy but everything should be in balance, and no food is intrinsically 'evil'.

- I would feel guilt about the friends and family I didn't pick up the phone to. Never sharing any responsibility with them, in that they hadn't rang me either and were probably not feeling the guilt that I was.

Then, there are deeper cuts of guilt:

- Guilt over not having more children, even though the one I had was everything we wanted and more.
- Guilt over experiencing the traumas I did and the impact on those I loved. Yes, it wasn't ideal, but was any of it my fault or initiated by me? No, therefore, there can be no guilt.
- Guilt over not being by Dad's side when he was fading and leaving his bedside on that last night (even though he knew he was loved beyond measure).
- Guilt over not acting as a carer for Mum, even though I fought tirelessly for appropriate care for her, and everyone assured me my decisions were wise.

These dilemmas, where guilt could have destroyed me slowly, have been resolved with peace. I once told someone recently that they didn't need to make me feel guilty because I do more than enough of that for myself. So, in the period of the most piercing grief when losing both parents, the crippling shackles have been broken free. For someone who self-critiques, wakes up in a blind panic about what I could have done differently, I can say for once that I am guilt-free.

After losing them, I felt a contentment that I had never experienced before. Before I get hurled with stones, I do miss them more than I ever thought I could. Every day, I get 'caught out' by things I want to tell them. When good things happen, the shine is slightly taken off it by the fact that I can't share it with them. Indeed, on a couple of occasions, I have rung Mum, knowing the line was disconnected months ago. But what has changed is my attitude towards myself. Having been (in the main) a dutiful daughter and knowing that I did everything I could for them over many years, now is my time. It has to be.

Lots of 'adult' children have told me that they feel the same aspect of relief, but it is not always acceptable to say that. There is a 'turning' point where the 'child' becomes the 'adult' and this juxtaposition is a heavy burden to carry. Especially if this coincides with the time when we should be gaining some freedom as our own children 'fly the nest'. The word 'martyr' is literally defined as 'someone who sacrifices something of great value' or 'voluntarily suffers death'. Would someone we love want any of us to suffer even more by being a martyr to the grief? I very much doubt it.

What are we to gain from constantly laying ourselves down on a bed of nails just so we can continue to suffer?

In the months after losing my second parent, I experienced every emotion imaginable, from raw pain to intense hyperactivity to restlessness to exhaustion to…calm. What I didn't experience was guilt. What I also experienced was joy. This feels like it should be a taboo—someone off work, still healing, but feeling happy. I was careful who I declared this to, but it was an absolute truth. I had been 'freed' of many things that were eroding who I was over at least seven years. I was able to properly rest at night, knowing I wasn't waiting for a phone call with more health concerns from my parents.

I was able to be on a break away, without having to dread a phone call which would bring more worry, or rushing the holiday along so I could return to caring. I was able to prioritise my own family, without it being at the expense of someone else. And ultimately, I was able to give myself time to evaluate what I needed. Time was the most precious commodity to me; I had never really valued or made use of it.

If my parents were the people I knew them to be, the parents I hope my husband and I are, there is no place on this planet where they would want me to be sad. It simply makes no sense.

I will have a constant piece of me that is missing—we were together for 46 and 51 years—so I do feel that loss always. But it is not to anyone's advantage to allow that grief to overwhelm me or dictate my future. So, if grief is the price we pay for love, surely, we can reframe this into: 'those we loved and grieved for, would want us to live again'.

I do not want anyone to ever think I would belittle their grief; there is no right way or wrong way, no timescale that is appropriate. Clearly, the loss of a parent is a very different context from the loss of a child or the sudden death of someone before their time. However, the most inspirational parents of children cruelly taken from them are the ones who channel their grief into charity work, raising awareness or helping others. For this is the best way for them to show their love for those they have lost. It is also what those they grieve, would want.

I have felt more intense grief when my beloved husband and daughter have been suffering mentally, and I couldn't fix them. We also have to remember to 'look after the living' rather than focusing on what we have lost.

For most of us, losing someone we love and who loved us is simply that…they are gone, but their love for us means we cannot be 'gone' too. We owe it to them to do the very opposite…to **live** fully, richly and with them in our hearts. Not forgotten but guiding us and most certainly guilt-free.

Don't Burst My Positivity Bubble!

I vividly remember a fellow colleague once defining me as 'annoyingly positive' in my role as a teacher. I was really quite stunned and later offended, as I am not sure positivity can ever be described as annoying!

Given some of life's challenges. I still retain my 'glass half-full' status, but clearly have had many moments where the glass was drained dry. This is part of life's rich tapestry, and no one can be positive all the time, but there is a reluctance on my part to accept others' negativity. In fact, the older I get, the more I will 'fight' it actively with positivity and will not give it an audience.

Numerous studies have been conducted on the positive impact on physical as well as mental health of adopting a optimistic outlook.

It's not 'rocket science' but:

- If you expect the day to be gloomy, it is likely that this will be manifested.
- If you feel you will fail a test/exam, your efforts to pass or succeed will be significantly reduced.
- If you feel there is no point in going out because rain is forecast, then you will miss the chance of glimmers of sunshine.

I don't aim to make this over-simplistic—there arc days, months, years when positive thinking takes every bit of energy. In recent years, the importance of dopamine and serotonin levels has been given a higher profile and is firmly rooted in research. What is less well known is that a daily practice of positive thinking can rewire the brain and will lead to 'brain plasticity'—basically, us being more resilient and adaptable.

As a mental health and well-being lead in a primary school, I studied many factors which could contribute to better mental wellness for our pupils. The most effective of these, in my opinion, was 'change your words, change your mindset'.

One of my biggest frustrations as a teacher and also a parent was when children would utter those immortal words, 'I can't do it!' One of the most significant shifts in the attitude of my class was when they started to say…'I can't do it yet!' This became commonplace language, and our job as educators was then made much easier by the fact that the learners had opened themselves up to the learning process. A gate had been opened rather than remaining firmly locked.

I spent many hours studying the work of Carol Dweck and others on 'Growth Mindset' and it is a truly fascinating area of psychological research for adults and children. Simply altering the way we word our responses and challenging our children to reframe their language is enormously effective. We can never develop into resilient adults if we don't accept that mistakes will be made on our journey, and that is okay.

I remember one tutor at college telling us that if a page full of Maths exercises had all ticks, this is more likely to show that no new learning is taking place, and the task was of insufficient challenge. This message has been at the core of my own practice, and the children all knew that they had to make mistakes in order to learn. That said, we must allow time for them to revisit what led to the error and explain how it can be 'fixed'. Surely, this analogy is true of how we view our own lives. Mistakes will be made, but as long as we learn what went wrong, take action and try our best not to repeat it, then this will only ever lead to growth.

I am also a fervent believer in allowing children to experience failure, as long as it is balanced with encouragement. All children may throw a board game across a room when they lose or kick a ball over the fence when they fail to score. It is normal to be disappointed. Taking children to sports events was, in some ways, one of the most challenging aspects of the job, especially when fielding a team significantly younger and smaller than the large schools we were competing with.

I would be the first to scream at full volume, encouraging hollers of support as a result of watching Nottingham Forest with my dad, believing that the louder I shout, the greater the chance of victory. I have continued this practice as a teacher on the sidelines at sports events, or a mum watching ladies' football and would still be prone to shedding a tear if my favourite team were to lose.

But every loss is an opportunity to learn.

The success and expertise of sports psychologists such as the renowned Steve Peters is something I hold in high esteem. Essentially, he states that 'the hidden chimp' will react with emotion and anger to loss, which is perfectly instinctive and normal. However, it needs managing through either professional intervention and support, allowing the emotions to run free, but then challenge them and reframe the mindset. His success is undeniable, and sometimes the evidence laid before you cannot be denied. If it works for celebrity fundraisers, athletes, snooker players and the like, it can work for us mere mortals.

We are relentlessly told by every expert in the media that we should train our bodies and stay physically strong. The time has come for us to train our minds in the same way for ultimate wellness.

Take the attitude of a student, never be too big to ask questions, never know too much to learn something new.

Maya Angelou

And Now To the End Of The Rainbow...There's A Land That I Yearned For

Ever since this multicoloured arc of beauty appeared over Noah's ark in Genesis, the rainbow has been viewed in our culture as a symbol of hope. But its symbolism reaches far deeper than that, and it is here where I turn for the last episode of this memoir. As each episode you have read ultimately sows seeds of hope in its reader, the rainbow seems a fitting end for a number of reasons.

Even in the darkest of times, when dark skies are all you can see, the power of light can work its magic and create this significant wonder. Lifting your spirits when you see it and showing that the dark skies won't last forever.

As children, many of us are intrigued by the notion of a pot of gold sitting invitingly at the end of it. Of course, our adult minds learn that this was never possible, as the rainbow is merely an optical effect. Just as we grow up to learn that there is no Father Christmas, our childhood beliefs are smashed to pieces. Pragmatic realists would say the rainbow is just a thing of science. But those of us with more spiritual beliefs would consider a double rainbow to be a meaningful sign sent to us at a time when we need it most.

I have seen these phenomena after losing a loved one, providing some sort of assurance that they will remain at my side, watching over me still, in the same way as that white feather which graced my path.

The rainbow has been depicted in artwork throughout many different styles and periods. Maybe the artists included it to draw the onlooker in and evoke a reaction of positivity. It also forms many a line of poetry, literature or song lyrics. From the likes of Dorothy from the Wizard of Oz to Bob Marley singing of *Rainbow Country*, where all colours, cultures are accepted and embraced with love, the rainbow remains a positive symbol. That said, in spite of the fact that this has been adopted in recent years as a badge of the LGBTQ+ community, some children will possibly grow up knowing a rainbow only for its symbolic representation of inclusivity, rather than of leprechauns and their pots of gold.

Finally, the term 'rainbow baby' is now used to describe and, in some way, soften the loss of a baby, when a later pregnancy results in joy and relief. Having had my own bundle of rainbow joy arrive in 2003, I know that she helped me realise there is a different plan afoot where grief can be soothed by new life, and this has shaped my view of trauma from that point on.

I am now going to approach a rainbow in a slightly different way. Bear with it and see if it can help you to consider everything life throws at us, with fresh eyes.

Red: There are times when either pure anger or even resentment can eat away at us. We can feel anger towards others for the way that they've behaved. And boy, have some people treated me like their worst enemy! Like a repelling magnet, if we encounter people with the opposite mindset and values to us, we can develop feelings which wish to oppose or confront them. In more extreme cases, we may wish them harm.

Possibly, the worst form of anger is that we can direct towards ourselves. We can be our own worst critics and beat ourselves up for the things we should have done (or did and then regret). Either way, anger is destructive, and once we ignite the match of anger, it can easily and quickly destroy. My 'short fuse' has lengthened considerably with maturity. I am far more likely to distance myself from anyone I may run the risk of getting angry with, and am far more willing to let things go.

I have also learnt that for some argumentative souls, they love to rile you, by evoking your anger and in giving it to them, they are getting the reaction that they sought.

Therefore, red for me is now being resigned to having to accept others' different opinions, even if they do not align with my own and mean I must, for once…step away.

Orange: As an amber traffic light warns us to either slow down or be poised to move, many of us like an element of preparation, being ready for what might come next. As an over-planner, I spent years where I yearned for the predictability of a full diary, wanting to know what was coming next. But life isn't always like that. It can throw us curve balls, which demand that we either slow down or change pace. Nothing can ever be truly in our control, and it has been refreshing to be able to catch those curve balls and run with them. We could view it as exciting to not know what is ahead of us, which we could not have predicted.

When I say, 'Be prepared', I'm not meaning in a Boy Scout fashion, always carrying a multi-tool and an emergency bar of Kendal Mint Cake! I mean that we are better to live our lives, accepting each day, but aware that we may need to adapt and expect the unexpected.

A life skill I have had to learn (not easy for a menopausal woman with ADHD!) is to be more flexible, and all the plans you have in the world could be thrown out of the window at any point. It is how resilient we are in dealing with these curves in the road or even crossroads, that matters.

Yellow: I could not imagine any other colour to represent joy. Sunshine, cornfields, a daffodil or a sunflower all bring joy courtesy of Mother Nature. For years, I was on a one-way track to success and work fulfilment, which I felt quite happy with in the main. I was trying to achieve the optimum in my career, but never allowed myself the opportunities for unplanned joy. I was capable of being happy when we planned a holiday, family event, etc., but there was no space to gaze at the sunset, smell the flowers and listen to what life can give us.

Don't get me wrong, many of the pupils I have taught over the years have granted me little pockets of sunshine, dispersed throughout the working day.

Nothing can quite make you smile like a funny quip, a word of childlike wisdom, or that affectionate hug a child will give you.

Pausing to sit beside mum for hours on end in her final weeks, almost every day…the sun shone. On the morning that she was to pass, I awoke to the most incredible sunrise I have ever seen. It was an image soon to be etched in my mind, accompanied by a song surrounding her last days and played at her funeral, *I watch the sunrise*. One of the lyrics will forever remain etched on my heart: *for you are always close to me, following all my ways*. That morning view, shining bright with warmth, brought me enormous comfort in those early days of grief. From that point on, I saw the sunrise as a different entity. Waking each morning, used to shooting out of bed with a feeling of doom and racing through every little bit of the day, was ruining my chance to see the optimism of a new dawn.

We owe it to ourselves to allow ourselves time to enjoy the sunshine and the joy, not just during an annual holiday…but every day.

Green: Easy to go for the 'green, green grass of home' for this one and to a certain degree, it is true. Growing up in a mining village, the iconic green hills overlooked many of my childhood memories. Equally, it could represent the hallowed turf of a football pitch, given that two of my favourite people in the world had a huge passion for the game, and many hours have been spent on the touchlines.

But in recent years, I have also developed an appreciation of nature and the beauty of a garden, which I never imagined was going to be a part of my 'life CV'! Taking time to ponder the fruits of my beloved Dad's green fingers led me to value the fact that my equally beloved husband seems to have the same magical touch with anything of the plant variety.

However, the theme of this book dictates that green in this context must represent… new growth. When the harsh, frozen days of winter give the smallest indications of hope, through the emerging snowdrops peeping through even the iciest ground, it fills you with optimism. For however harsh our winters might be (both real and metaphorical), warmer days will come, and this will always lead to new growth.

None of us is a finished article. We need to be shaped, crafted and nurtured in order for us to be the best versions of ourselves. It may be a cliché, but this happens at the times when we are challenged to such a point that we don't think we will ever recover. But we do. Life gives us a chance to grow in a slightly different direction, and when tended with care, we can blossom into something more beautiful than before.

Green for me has almost meant 'Go' like the traffic light. Go for what you yearn for. Go, when to stay is too difficult, and it is time. Go where you feel you are being led. And don't reverse backwards!

BLUE: My favourite colour has always been blue. It is not a colour I have ever viewed as masculine. Why is blue just for the boys?

What do you think of when you see blue? I am sure 90% of us would say either sky or sea. The vastness of both of these can at times feel daunting, but I see calm. I doubt there is anything better than lying on the sand, gazing at a cobalt blue cloud-free sky. The enormity of what is above us is magnified by a tiny white plane trail, scoring its mark through the blanket of blue.

A spectrum of azure, turquoise and cerulean blues glisten within the rippling waves. Yes, we know the sea can be a thing of danger and is not to be underestimated for its power.

But as I recounted my beloved Bridlington, thc sight of it will forever fill me with excitement and ultimately peace. There is no sound I would rather hear than the ripple of the waves. From holding a conch shell to my ear, at home in landlocked Nottingham, I would yearn for that noise as a child. I would wish for this to be the final sound I hear when my time on this mortal coil is over. My heaven would have a sea in it for sure. It is not just its array of colour, its clarity, its soothing sway; it has far deeper connotations for me.

For oceans and rivers run deep—as do I. There is a beauty in the unknown and what you can't see under the surface. On my 'surface', I can 'come across wrong', having had to develop a tough, 'don't mess' exterior with an inner motor on overdrive. It has been said on more than one occasion that I may be classed as 'high maintenance'. In reality, I am multi-layered if you dive deeper. Within me, there is an ocean of complexities, both beautiful and dangerous. Could the same not be said about the sea? But diving in with me is usually worth it! So, my advice would be…

Never be afraid of diving deeply and gazing up!

Indigo: That same sky of cobalt blue looks equally as stunning when dotted with diamond-like stars. Indigo skies wrap us up in a blanket, inducing slumber. Night skies for me are not black; they are purple-tinged with a velvety richness. The wonder of constellations has alluded me for a lifetime, but when someone more learned than I pointed out the formation of 'The Plough', I was mystified. Not just by the star formations, but also by him! For someone who can try to understand the 'unfathomable' expanse of space, could surely make sense of the aspects of me that are certainly at times, also incomprehensible.

I don't pretend to be a physician or an astronomer, but I do know that 'my mind is blown' by what shines down on us mere mortals at night. It constantly both baffles and astounds me. We are so incredibly small and seemingly insignificant when compared to the stratosphere, but to those we hold dear, we are their entire world. I can only imagine how the likes of Tim Peake can resume normal life: the school run, the supermarket shop, watching TV, etc, when they have previously looked down on our immense earth as a tiny dot.

How could life ever be the same again? In a similar way to experiencing a near-death experience or being the sole survivor from an air disaster, you just have to embrace your place and your timing in the world. There is a plan at work greater than we know or could comprehend, yet at times, we still believe we are the main controller.

Therefore, I will continue to look up to the indigo sky and realise my insignificance but also my worth, that I am still here and have my place in this universe.

Violet: For the final colour of the rainbow, I conclude with one of the main influences throughout my life, both positive and at times, negative, but without this, my life would certainly have had less sparkle within it. The purple, pink hues are my female 'sisters': My friends. As I recounted earlier, not all of these have proved to be winter friends, enduring year after year, withstanding distance, time or turmoil. But I still treasure every one of them, from the very first, who loved me for the mad craziness of my youth, to the winter friends who have held me through parenthood, illness and grief.

Those who see you for all your flaws and witness your brutally raw emotions, yet can still laugh with you, be silly with you and remind you that being 51 doesn't mean you can't still be a big kid. For me, these friends have been solely female. I know many women value a platonic friendship with a man, but for me, I had the best male friend I could have had in my dad. We could wile away hours spent talking, walking and drinking wine. He possessed an instinctive knowledge of the way I 'ticked' and his unconditional love, which was ever-present, is a loss I will always carry—for no one will ever quite be able to fill that particular hole.

The symbolism of violet is one of spirituality and creativity, and this makes it the perfect choice to sit at the end of my rainbow.

Without spirituality at my core, guiding me throughout my life, and people around me who embrace this, I doubt I would have been able to navigate my survival and recovery.

Without creativity, I wouldn't be here now. My need to create something meaningful for others was fulfilled for many years by my teaching career, echoing the legacy my mum left for me. My creativity sat within every lesson plan, every display, every story told to a class of open-mouthed babes. It now sits within the words that are before you on this page. My inner writer has been locked away for long enough, and it has been a joy to share this with you.

I want you urge you, reader, that this is just the beginning. For you and for me. Remember, every day is a chance for that clean slate. Thank you for giving me the chance to start afresh and holding my hand through it all.

Be a rainbow in someone else's cloud.

Maya Angelou

Useful Links

Dealing with grief:
Home – The Good Grief Trust

Post-natal depression/ baby loss:
PANDAS Foundation UK

Mental wellbeing:
Suicide Prevention Charity | Campaign Against Living Miserably
We're Mind, the mental health charity | Mind
Papyrus UK Suicide Prevention | Prevention of Young Suicide
3 Dads Walking
YoungMinds | Mental Health Charity For Children And Young People | YoungMinds
Suicide Prevention Charity | Campaign Against Living Miserably

Outdoor swimming:
Outdoor Swimmer - Wild Swimming News, Features, Gear and Tips

Eating Disorders:
The UK's Eating Disorder Charity - Beat
Educational settings/ support:
Education Support, supporting teachers and education staff

Health issues:
Stroke Association | Strength through support
https://www.hospiceuk.org/
https://www.mariecurie.org.uk/information

ADHD/ Neurodiversity:

Sanctum Healthcare | ADHD, Autism & Brain Health Clinic | Cheshire

https://adhduk.co.uk/

Epilogue

The box sits in the middle of the room where I once slept.
It is dusty, battered and bruised, sealed barely with ageing yellow Sellotape.
It is unfamiliar to me, but so insignificant and mundane in appearance.
Inside the box are remnants of a life once lived, a youth misspent, a childhood blurred into teenage turmoil, a career forged, relationships both nurtured and neglected, illnesses both overcome and succumbed to.
I close the box.

The box sits under the cherry blossom tree in the garden.
It is wooden, solid, with a perfectly fitted lid, made of rosewood.
It is not like any other box I have ever seen.
Its beauty and togetherness draw me in.
Inside the box are notes of hope. Whispers of positivity and bubbles of excitement drift to the surface. A bright future radiates out where there is…
space to grow,
space to be free and space to be me.
I open the box.

Acknowledgements

Acknowledgements to those who know already and those who were part of this 'story'.

This part is a lot harder to write than the rest of the book. Why?

Because when you look back on your life so far, at 51, and think about who has influenced you and who has shaped the narrative, the list would be endless. Every relationship or even encounter, however lasting or brief, has played its part. But here we are… and there are some lights of my life that shine too bright to ignore.

This book is Mum and Dad's story as much as it is mine. They were not only my parents but also my friends. They gave me the foundations on which to build my own small but imperfectly formed and beautiful family.

First and foremost, this book would never have been started had my strong, independent mum, who very much knew her own mind, been lying dying, ravaged by cancer in her last four weeks of life. Thank you to her for giving me permission to follow my dream and leave teaching in order to possess the headspace and to jump off the treadmill. We had conversations in those last four weeks which we maybe should have had earlier, but we laughed, we cried and we grew 100 times closer. Heartfelt thank yous to all the friends and family who visited her in those last four weeks for showing her how much you loved her.

None of that would have been possible without the incredible nursing home and the staff who became family – I will never forget them or the experience we had there.

Dad – well… where to begin? He always said 'he had a book in him', and he never sat down to write it. This is for him. He was eloquent, creative, inspiring and my best friend in the whole world. He knew how I was feeling the minute he walked in the room and **always** thought I was beautiful, even when I was at my lowest. He was the reason I knew I had to overcome any of the mental health battles, because he had overcome far worse and I would never willingly have made him sad. The grief I feel for them both could so easily have overwhelmed me, but they are with me every day, and their shared faith and belief that one day we will be reunited is something I am eternally thankful for. All those Sunday evening strolls to The Moor Chapel must have paid off!

I have said this in an earlier chapter, but I simply feel very lucky in meeting my soulmate. Meeting my partner in 'crime' was a chance meeting, which then sealed my future. He simply is 'my best friend' and 'the love of my life' (to coin his two favourite Queen songs!). His never-ending patience in coping with me can never be underestimated. I'm not quite sure how he has done it, but I'm sure glad he did! We are stronger in our love every day and will hold hands until 'him upstairs' calls us home. He makes me laugh, sees my inner beauty and, whilst he may not have understood my 'need' to write, has allowed me the time and afforded me the opportunity to chase my lifetime's ambition. He's a good one! And Mum loved him enormously too!

She will be highly embarrassed to read this, but hey ho! What else should mums do but embarrass their children? I am immensely proud to be a mum of one. She was everything we needed and ever wanted and has never disappointed. Far from it! She has a backbone of steel which will serve her very well, and I know she is destined for great things! I hope one day she will read this and know that her mum was a fighter who could always 'fix' things. I know with certainty that I may be very flawed but have learnt to know my worth, and she must know hers.

To my Winter friends – you know who you are. You know how much I love you all, and you have 'had my back' on many occasions and seen me move through many of these challenges. You have answered the phone at midnight to uncontrollable sobbing in the pit of grief and not let go.

You have listened to the same words and the same problems, without judgement or boredom!

You have taken me out, got me drunk, and we have laughed till we cried.

You have made me feel young again when I actually felt ancient, and we still plan on sitting in that care home with a stash of good wine, laughing with childlike freedom.

And finally, to all the teachers who have shaped me, both in the classroom and out of it. Both the teachers who I sat in front of and the teachers I was privileged to work alongside. It is fair to say that the teachers we encounter can be a very mixed bag, but the gems amongst them leave a sparkle in your life which never fades. I was lucky to have 'fallen' into teaching, even though it was against my better judgement at the time. There are no regrets, and I hope I have left even the smallest of impressions. It is a profession to be proud of and should be valued far more than it is.

The final thank you goes to the pupils who had Miss Greaves (and the married version) for their memorable characters, their 'spark', their willingness to go along with the 'mad' teacher who stood in front of them and the way they laid themselves bare at times. Again, those pupils will know who they are; I am blessed to have them still in my life as adults, and they were all a part of my wider family and my story.

And reader… whoever you are, wherever you are going, there is always hope, there is always someone to listen, and change is most certainly a good thing.